American Realist Fictions of Marriage

MODERN
AMERICAN
LITERATURE
New Approaches

Yoshinobu Hakutani
General Editor

Vol. 68

This book is a volume in a Peter Lang monograph series.
Every volume is peer reviewed and meets
the highest quality standards for content and production.

PETER LANG
New York • Bern • Frankfurt • Berlin
Brussels • Vienna • Oxford • Warsaw

Kelli V. Randall

American Realist Fictions of Marriage

From Kate Chopin, Edith Wharton to Frances Harper, Pauline Hopkins

PETER LANG
New York • Bern • Frankfurt • Berlin
Brussels • Vienna • Oxford • Warsaw

Library of Congress Cataloging-in-Publication Data

Names: Randall, Kelli V., author.
Title: American realist fictions of marriage: from Kate Chopin, Edith Wharton to Frances Harper, Pauline Hopkins / Kelli V. Randall.
Description: New York: Peter Lang, 2017.
Series: Modern American literature: new approaches; v. 68 | ISSN 1078-0521
Includes bibliographical references and index.
Identifiers: LCCN 2017019792 | ISBN 978-1-4331-2868-4 (hardcover: alk. paper)
ISBN 978-1-4539-1478-6 (ebook pdf) | ISBN 978-1-4331-4431-8 (epub)
ISBN 978-1-4331-4432-5 (mobi)
Subjects: LCSH: Marriage in literature.
American fiction—19th century—History and criticism.
American fiction—20th century—History and criticism.
American fiction—Women authors—History and criticism.
Classification: LCC PS374.M35 R36 2017 | DDC 813.009/3543
LC record available at https://lccn.loc.gov/2017019792
DOI 10.3726/978-1-4539-1478-6

Bibliographic information published by **Die Deutsche Nationalbibliothek**. **Die Deutsche Nationalbibliothek** lists this publication in the "Deutsche Nationalbibliografie"; detailed bibliographic data are available on the Internet at http://dnb.d-nb.de/.

Cover photo courtesy of the author.

The paper in this book meets the guidelines for permanence and durability of the Committee on Production Guidelines for Book Longevity of the Council of Library Resources.

29 Broadway, 18th floor, New York, NY 10006
www.peterlang.com

Printed in Germany

For my father, Charles Roy Randall. Gone but not forgotten.

Table of Contents

Preface

American Realist Fictions of Marriage intervenes in the field of American literary realism by arguing that selected marriage fiction of Kate Chopin, Frances Harper, Pauline Hopkins, Williams Dean Howells, Emma Dunham-Kelly, and Edith Wharton interrogates the possibility of harmonious societies based on racial, gender, and social equality. *Megda* (1891), *An Imperative Duty* (1891), *Iola Leroy* (1892), *The Awakening* (1899), *Contending Forces* (1900), and *The House of Mirth* (1905) express suspicion about marriage and its potential consequences. These six novels use marriage as a forum to explore the problem of the "color line," sexism, and class difference that promoted social boundaries. These novels demonstrate how choices about marriage made by female protagonists are metaphorical representations of social equality while simultaneously revealing threats to that ideal vision. *American Realist Fictions of Marriage* explores the ways marriage infringes upon protagonists' development into autonomous women in imperfect societies.

Marriage holds a distinct place in the American cultural imagination, and it is an important index of female identity in the Age of

Realism. *American Realist Fictions of Marriage* intervenes in current critical debates in American literary realism by showing how realism functions as a mode of narration for fictive constructions of marriage and the race, gender, and class upheavals these depictions of marriage represent. In a wider context, *American Realist Fictions of Marriage* aims to widen the conventional narrow focus on canonical realist writers by highlighting intellectual exchanges that were taking place between traditional and nontraditional writers about marriage.

Acknowledgments

I did not craft this book alone. While working to bring this project to fruition, I received a great deal of support from colleagues, family, and friends. First, I would like to acknowledge Mr. Zeus Preckwinkle of Chicago, Illinois, my 4th and 6th grade teacher, who instilled in me very early on a love for both reading and writing. I would like to thank members of the Ervin and Randall families who provided me with invaluable support and encouragement when I needed it most. For intellectual support and encouragement, I am grateful to Dr. Michael A. Elliott, Dr. Frances Smith Foster, Dr. Christine Levenduski, and Dr. Carla J. Mulford. I owe a special thanks to Dr. Sharma, Dr. Erwin, Dr. Vickers, and Dr. Callahan for their supportive friendship over the years. I owe a special debt of gratitude to my mother, Shervia Jean Ervin Randall for her generous monetary gifts and invaluable prayers, wisdom, and encouragement. Mommy, you have always been and will always be my biggest supporter. Finally, I extend my deepest appreciation to my deceased father, Charles Roy Randall. Gone but never forgotten. Daddy, I am forever indebted to you, for you encouraged me from the very beginning until your end. Even in your absence now, your spirit of love, encouragement, and support abounds.

Introduction

Realism and the Value of Marriage on an American Scene

The Age of Realism commonly refers to a period of realist writing from approximately 1865 to 1910. Emerging as a technique of novel writing after the Civil War and becoming a distinct genre by the 1880s, realism was in conversation with other competing modes of representation and cultural practices. Realism emerged after the Civil War, a time of healing and restoring.[1] Some realist fiction of this period depicts marriage as a means of healing and reconciliation on individual, communal, and even national levels. Many changes were occurring in the world, including Reconstruction, the modern scientific revolution, the industrial revolution, migration from rural to urban environments, and high rates of immigration. Realists felt it was their own ethical responsibility to tell the truth about the common everyday life of ordinary people, and they prided themselves in objectively depicting ordinary middle and lower class life in literature that interrogated cultural difference. "Realism was just as much a way of seeing as a set of texts, and those ways of seeing permeated the entire culture through indirect borrowings, common material, and social expectations."[2] Characters in realist novels are products of social factors. Their environments play key parts in the dramatic complications that can occur, particularly in social constructions of consumerism that require characters to make moral and ethical decisions.

Realism was a subject of controversy in its own time, and debates occurred about the suitability of realism as a mode of representation. Concerns about novel reading and novel writing were deeply engrained in the political consciences and literary imaginations of many realist writers. Some realists felt it was their responsibility to both outline their writing philosophies and justify their writing practices. "Fidelity to everyday life and to probability of motive were easy to theorize about than to realize."[3] As a result, many realists often violated theories they claimed to practice in their novels.

William Dean Howells, the lone male author included in *American Realist Fictions of Marriage*, is nicknamed the "Dean of American Letters"[4] Howells has an economic vision of realism. "As the spokesman for American realism, Howells uses the terms economy and excess to advertise proportionate views of the world to correct the falsifying, excessive vision of the sentimental."[5] Howells describes realism as "nothing more and nothing less than the truthful treatment of material."[6] Furthermore, realism depicts "'the simple, the natural, and the honest.'"[7] "Simple," "natural," and "honest" are classic terms of Howellsian realism.[8] Howells has poignant instructions for realist writers: "We must ask ourselves before we ask anything else, Is it true?—true to the motives, the impulses, the principles that shape the life of actual men and women?"[9] According to Howells, realist writers have a responsibility to adhere to the tenants of the genre realism. Presenting life as it is and not as the author wants it to be is vitally important for realists. Howells considers realism the superior tradition to be taken more seriously than the romance and sentimental. "More specifically, Howells's endorsement of the 'economy' of realism consistently included a critique of the 'excess' of romance and sentiment"[10] Romantic and sentimental conventions predicate an excess of emotion and sympathy that Howells does not envision for realism. On the other hand, realism seeks "to achieve a balanced economy within a balanced formal structure"[11] Yet even Howells is conflicted in his philosophies on writing.

Like a number of realists, he adheres to and also violates theories regarding the function of literature.

Defining realism was a difficult task for writers during the Age of Realism itself, and it remains a difficult task for contemporary scholars of literary realism now. Today, debates surrounding realism still continue. "No genre—if it can be called a genre—is more difficult to define than realism, and this is particularly true of American realism."[12] The enticing nature of falling into the trap of collapsing realism, the literary movement, into "realistic," the adjective, explains why it is so difficult to pin down an accurate definition of realism. If something is described as realistic, it is considered to be an accurate portrayal unclouded by false ideals. According to the *Webster's II New Riverside Dictionary*, realism is "concern with facts and things as they actually are; the depiction of reality."[13] Yet as Walter Benn Michaels has long argued, "Realism, defined by its fidelity to things as they are, can never in principle serve as a model, good or bad, since only when art is *not* like life can life attempt to be like art."[14] Realists write to instruct more so than to entertain their audiences. Realist writing is not confined by literary convention or aesthetics. Mimetic, matter-of-fact, and straightforward, realist writing prides itself on verisimilitude. A literary technique of writing practiced by many schools of writing, realism had multiple relationships with other competing modes of writing. Circles of romantics, realists, and naturalists debated ways fictional characters should be represented in relation to the external world. Many novelists often blended other techniques of writing with realism as a solution to the debate.

Nancy Bentley's *Ethnography of Manners* argues that novel writing is a social practice. In her study of novels written by Nathaniel Hawthorne, Henry James, and Edith Wharton, Bentley demonstrates that fiction writing is a practice akin to "mastering manners on the page."[15] Bentley argues that "convergences between novels and ethnographic texts" aid in the production of "our modern discourse of culture."[16] The locus of culture is an appropriate place to begin defining and contextualizing realism. To successfully define realism, it will be necessary to work from a clear understanding of realism as a literary movement, realism as an institution bound by particular values and aesthetics, realism as a mode of writing in the novel genre, and realism as a contemporary area of scholarship critically focused on a set of canonical writers. One way to begin thinking about this issue is to revise the modern critical assumption that realism was a white, patriarchal dominated genre that specifically promoted white male bourgeois values and western perspectives.[17] This assessment solely reflects a popular trend in current American literary realist scholarship that misconstrues the realist era as constricted and segregated. More exciting approaches to scholarship consider the dialogues and intellectual exchanges that were already taking place between canonical and non-canonical writers of the era.

Most definitions by contemporary scholars tend to offer vague and confusing descriptions of what realism really is. What most scholars have not done is define the fate of realism as a technique, subject matter, genre of writing, and form of representation within the context of American literary history. As technique, subject matter, and a representation of middle-class life, René Wellek refers to realism as "the objective representation of contemporary social reality."[18] Wellek's revered definition of realism still leaves two unanswered questions: what does it mean to be objective in representation and what is contemporary social reality? Wellek's definition simply puts forth "a period concept" or prescription for late-nineteenth-century American and European literature.[19] However, this definition is important because it discredits the popular misconception of realism as an independent genre.

There are a number of ongoing scholarly debates and critical studies of realism. Many of these critical studies attempt to explain what realism is, why it came about, and why it is useful. Warner Berthoff begins *The Ferment of Realism* with the following statement: "The great collective event in American letters during the 1880s and 1890s was the securing of 'realism' as the dominant standard of value."[20] Berthoff uses the term realism to periodize a specific literary history containing the canonical writers William Dean Howells, Mark Twain, and Henry James. Berthoff avoids the appropriation of the word "realism" to describe a specific mode or genre of writing. He instead places the word "realism" in quotations to reference the problem of the term "realism" itself. For Berthoff, realism is the increased motive and usage of expression, which responds to the social, political, and economic changes occurring during 1884–1919. Realism is a broad response to social changes taking place such as industrialism, market economy, and segregation of classes. From this perspective, socio-political changes and historical events have primary emphasis of focus over texts, which supposedly reflect those realities. Less emphasis is placed upon the literary conventions of texts.

New historicist critics such as Daniel Borus, June Howard, Walter Benn Michaels, and Amy Kaplan challenge literary-historicized critical texts by Berthoff, Edwin Cady (*The Road to Realism*), and Donald Pizer (*Realism and Naturalism in Nineteenth-Century American Literature*) by suggesting that realist novels are not solely reactions or responses to social and political changes. New historicists argue that realism is a literal part of the ongoing shifts in society and culture. The literary histories of canonical realist works are important for they offered early definitions of realist works and determined the worth of realist texts. Borus, Michaels, Howard, and Kaplan's work differ from the literary histories of realism because they ask historical questions as related to literary texts. In *Writing Realism*, Daniel Borus describes the realist writer's goal to create "a common culture in which all classes could partake."[21] Thus, realism has a social function in a democratic society.

Some critics have defined realism as a democratizing of literature. Alfred Habeggar finds "the positive side of American realism" to be "its vision of democratic action."[22] Realism then becomes a realization of democracy. From this perspective, realism was a movement that did something to the overall scope of literature politically. "Works of fiction were considered as expressions of the general impulse toward the democratization of American letters."[23] As a result, realism had the power to impact social progress. To this end, Michele Birnbaum defines realism by the conventions it employed and by the subsequent effects, these conventions had upon the realist novel's ability to both explain the world and accomplish something in the world. She writes, "Literary realism always depends on narrative convention, caricature, cliché, and affectation in its effort to make manageable an unmanageable world."[24] Various conventions of realism such as detailed and journalistically descriptive passages in realist novels were the realist writer's attempt to pin down reality and make the unfamiliar real.

Walter Benn Michaels explains the goal of new historicist critics. He writes, "The only relation literature as such has to culture as such is that it is part of it."[25] For new historicists, realist texts are a central part of the historical moment, various cultural shifts, and socio-political realities. In *The Gold Standard and the Logic of Naturalism*, Michaels's goal is to "map out the reality in which a certain literature finds its place."[26] By contrast, Amy Kaplan wants to "recuperate realism's relation to social change not as a static background which novels either naively record or heroically evade, but as the foreground of the narrative structure of each novel" in her critical study *The Social Construction of American Realism*.[27] June Howard aims to "trace how naturalism is shaped by and imaginatively reshapes a historical experience that, although it exists outside representation and narrative, we necessarily approach through texts" in her critical work *Form and History in American Literary Naturalism*.[28]

All three of these critical studies refute the use of the term "realism" as a generic label. Howard and Michaels do away with the term altogether and use the less-problematic term "naturalism."[29] Kaplan uses the term "realism" to describe a movement and mark a period of writing commonly referred to as the Age of Realism. Michael Davitt Bell critiques the practice of labeling literary periods such as realism and naturalism because these terms became containers for writers largely associated within a single literary tradition. In *The Problem of American Realism*, Bell argues that it is virtually impossible to come up with a consistent definition of realism or naturalism to encompass various writers' agendas and the content of their works. While Bell does not advocate a solution to "the problem of American realism," he does suggest that scholars must be mindful of the fact that writers, "whether or not they proclaimed themselves to be realists or naturalists," had to contend with a seriously problematic conception of literary realism."[30]

Realism has also been defined as the objective representation of urban middle-class life in the novel. These depictions are usually characterized by journalistic, scientific detail, coded diction, and middle-class cultural values are privileged. While this definition specifies that realism centered upon discussions of urban middle-class life, it remains vague about the cultural values and coded diction. Class, like race, is also defined on an evolutionary chain of being. "Realism's fidelity to the details of contemporary, everyday life almost required that those authors document class structure, define the 'fittest' within class conflicts, and reveal the injustices perpetuated on the poor by the rich."[31] Realist novels often accommodate the interests and aspirations of an insurgent middle class. Cuddy argues that realist novels that dealt with conflicts between classes often fell prey to Darwinian discourse.

However, realists were not confident in fiction's ability to portray the real world. Though the social purpose of literature mandated that literature had become commodity for consumption, it is dangerous to view realism solely in terms of the world it claimed to represent. "Mass culture may not have completely copied realism, but it shared certain preoccupations of representation and subject matter."[32] Incidentally, realists were not confident in fiction's ability to portray the real world because they distrusted the social. In The *Social Construction of American Realism*, Kaplan describes realism as a social construction or expression of consumer culture. She makes the distinction between realism on a real world level and fictional level. In Kaplan's estimation, realism is in conversation with competing modes of representation. Realism is also in competition with popular fiction, mass printing, and other cultural practices. Kaplan argues, "Realists do more than passively record the world outside; they actively create and criticize the meanings, representations, and ideologies of their own changing culture."[33] Kaplan describes how realist writers use realism as strategy for defining their own social position as authors. Writers use realism as a strategy for imagining and handling threats of social change. As a result, realism most always expresses an anxiety, urgency, and evasiveness about the unpredictability of middle-class life.

Perhaps there is a direct relationship between the urgency realist writers express and the vague definitions applied in hopes of understanding realism now. Elizabeth Ammons often argues that circular definitions of realism will persist until we deal with the fact that realism as a mode of writing and literary movement is white patriarchal centered. Ammons writes, "When we say American realism, two immediate questions are: Whose reality? And: Whose America?"[34] Her quote suggests that realism is a white, patriarchal genre that specifically promotes white male bourgeois values and western perspectives. When staking such a claim, it is necessary to carefully distinguish between the literary movement realism, the genre realism, and the contemporary form of scholarship American literary realism. It is American literary realism, a contemporary area of scholarship that defines realism as a movement dominated by white men.

During the Age of Realism, the realist movement was most likely not considered a movement exclusive to white men. If anything, the idea of realism as a club of white men reflects a popular trend in current literary realist scholarship. Elizabeth Ammons's article shows that realism as a movement is not as exclusive as we think. The undeniable reality of multiplicity in experience and multi-vocal perspective during the Age of Realism compels her to call for an expansion of the American realist canon. Ammons is right in her demand for an interrogation of the contemporary canon of authors. While some contemporary scholars popularize the notion of realism as a constricted bubble of white men, more exciting approaches are looking at the dialogues and intellectual exchanges that were already taking place between those we now call traditional realists and those writers less traditionally included in the era. Unfortunately, the contemporary canon of realism now continues to impose limitations on dialogues between untraditional pairings of authors and conversations between seemingly opposing texts.

Nancy Glazener's *Reading for Realism: The History of a U. S. Literary Institution, 1850–1910* makes an important contribution to this ongoing debate and reinvestigation of the American literary realist canon. She considers the manner in which the *Atlantic* group of magazines affected critical attitudes about realism and novel-reading practices.

Glazener makes the compelling argument that audiences of readers actually influenced the production of various literary forms. If expectations of readers and their perceived values of literature shaped the genre of realism during the Age, contemporary expectations of scholars and their definitions of literary value influence who is in and who is out of the canon. Glazener's work points at the manner in which realism has and continues to serve elitist structures of class and power.

What I have attempted to do is different in both method and outcome from any of these critical works in the preceding critical genealogy of realism. A number of critical studies have been particularly useful for the formulation of my arguments about the relationship between realism and marriage. The critical scholarship of realism enables me to argue that a number of realist novels offer historical representations of marriage as closely intertwined with patriarchy. Marriage is a patriarchal institution, which lends itself to realism's novelistic discussions of racism, sexism, and class. Realism's representations of marriage encourage feminist critiques of the institution's reinforcement of hierarchies between men and women, blacks and whites, and varying social classes.

Rather than incorporating a literary history of realism or a new historicist theoretical approach to realism, I have studied realism within a framework of the marriage fiction of Kate Chopin, Frances Harper, Pauline Hopkins, William Dean Howells, Emma Kelley, and Edith Wharton. By this I mean my central question is not whether or not each novel I have selected is a realist novel, as it is largely for literary historians and new historicist critics who seek to map out definitions of realism, label bodies of works as realist, compare and contrast features and conventions of realism in various works, and place certain texts squarely within the realist canon. I consider the manner in which *Megda* (1891), *An Imperative Duty* (1891), *Iola Leroy* (1892), *The Awakening* (1899), *Contending Forces* (1900), and *The House of Mirth* (1905) inscribe and disrupt traditional views of marriage. The concerns of my study are to demonstrate that marriage is a worthy topic of attention in American literary realist studies. My own study attempts to show that marriage, as evidenced within the fiction of the writers I have selected, holds a distinct place in American cultural imagination. It has often been said that literature mirrors society by cleansing or indicting the American national conscience. Some realist novels pose uncomfortable questions about social justice, class-standing, racial equality, and gender equality, which lie at the center of our national experiences as Americans.

Critics such as Amy Kaplan have defined realism as an expression of the middle class. While realism is often referred to as an expression of high culture because of its focus on urban middle-class life and values, the middle-class based its identity upon what it affirmed and rejected. Incidentally, most realist writers were urban middle-class people, but they drew their identities from what they were not: lower class, upper class, immigrants, and blacks. For this reason, we find many negative and stereotyped references to marginalized groups of people in realist novels. While there are often discussions in realist texts about blacks, women, and immigrants, these references tend to be pejorative or stereotyped depictions.

A large body of scholarly critical works on the racial scientific thought and racial discourse of the late-nineteenth century substantiates why realist writers appropriated racial discourses in their depictions of blacks, immigrants, or lower-class members of society. John Haller's *Outcasts from Evolution: Scientific Attitudes of Racial Inferiority* traces intellectual thought from 1859 to 1900 that led to the emergence of American racial scientific theories and attitudes. His study clearly lays out "race" vocabulary and concepts, which developed from science that justified and rationalized "the value system upon which the idea of racial inferiority rested in American thought."[35] A similar work, *The Black Image in the White Mind: The Debate on Afro-American Character and Destiny,* details the debates surrounding the destiny and character of African Americans. George Frederickson argues that "differing predictions made about the ultimate destiny of American blacks reveal much about essential white attitudes."[36] Frederickson further explores what he calls "the tragic limitation of the white racial imagination of the nineteenth-century."[37] He highlights the white racial imagination's inability to see and failure to articulate a racially homogenous American society.

Similarly, Cathy Boeckmann's *A Question of Character: Scientific Racism and the Genres of American Fiction* examines the influence of racialized language upon nineteenth-century theories of racial difference. This scholarly work clarifies the connections between race, language, and scientific thought during the mid-to-late-nineteenth-century. Boeckmann also maps the role that race plays in genres and conventions of literature. She locates, "discourse of character squarely within the development of American literary realism."[38] Lee Baker also suggests that racial categories and racial constructs that seem stable are always in a constant state of flux. *From Savage to Negro* traces the shifting discourses of race in the United States from 1896 to 1954. This scholarly work explores the specific relationship between discourses on race within anthropology and rapidly changing racial constructs in order to show that the two have influenced one another. Baker argues, "Racial categories are produced and reproduced ideologically and culturally: they are constructed."[39] In addition, I would add that racial categories are also deconstructed.

Kenneth Warren's *Black and White Strangers* is an example of a critical study, which explodes and expands the realist canon by showing the connections between race and realism. Warren's work reveals that "concerns about 'race' may structure our American texts, even when those texts are not 'about' race in any substantive way."[40] Warren's work sets black novels in conversation with realist texts traditionally labeled as canonical. His study attempts to do away with current methods of studying black and white authors as strangers. Warren's critical work demonstrates partnerships between unlikely pairings of black and white texts. To have only white texts in the realist canon is only part of the equation. In depth examinations of the works of Henry James and William Dean Howells in Warren's *Black and White Strangers* reveals more about the "nadir" and the conversations between the black and white texts written during this period.[41] Warren argues that without blacks, immigrants, and lower class members there would be no American realism. These individuals provide both subject matter for realist novels and a measuring stick for middle-class realists to define themselves against. Kenneth Warren suggests that "realism can only evade or falsify the true nature of black 'reality' and American racism."[42] He argues that the place of realism in African American literature of the post-bellum era has been treated with suspicion. Warren argues that anxieties and concerns of race structured American works that appear to be most overtly not about race.

Realism was a movement that did something to the overall scope of literature politically because it had the power to impact social progress. Because truth is often stranger than fiction, some realist novelists made visible that which could not so easily be seen about race relations, class distinctions, and gender relations.[43] Many realist novels describe American life based upon its economic concerns, sexism, and racism. These various social conditions generate circumstances of suffering. Wai-Chee Dimock states, "Understood as such, suffering never exists in isolation, but always in partnership with something else. It is only half the equation, as it were, in an economy of pain, the other half being not only its complement but also its compensation."[44] Dimock argues that suffering is the "real," and this is evident in the objective descriptions of industrialism, capitalism, racism, and sexism in realist novels. Dimock writes, "Suffering ennobles, then, precisely because, by virtue of the loss that it entails, it is also able to bring forth a new ratio in one's composition of character, a new balance of attributes, and a gain commensurate with the loss."[45] Suffering builds moral character, and realist novels often express high regard for moral and ethical behavior. More importantly, the depiction of suffering in realist novels offers comfort for audiences of readers who must contend with their own forms of "real" life suffering.

Toni Morrison aims to shift discussions of race as an interrogation of "black" suffering to interrogations of power and status associated with whiteness. In *Playing in the Dark*, Morrison asserts that the American nation suffers a great injustice by extracting racial politics from its literary criticism. Morrison's slim volume provides a useful theoretical lens for discussing race in American literature. Her three essays indict literary criticism for its failure to interrogate whiteness and blackness appropriately in canonical works such as Edgar Allen Poe's *The Narrative of Arthur Gordon Pym* (1835), Mark Twain's *Huckleberry Finn* (1885), and Willa Cather's *Sapphira and the Slave Girl* (1940). Ultimately, Morrison argues that this avoidance of discussions of race, or the "Africanist presence" in American literature, is to deny that which has been instrumental in shaping the nation's history.[46] Similar to Morrison's examination of multiculturalism, Eric Sundquist's *To Wake the Nations* discusses the influence of African Americans on American literature. Sundquist, like Morrison, argues that the influence penetrates our culture to such a great extent that it cannot be removed from any serious study of American literature.

Realists are interested in examining social relations or patterns of social behavior. Their novels focus upon relationships between people in a given social context, and marriage is the quintessential social relation. Though this is a literary study of writers on the subject of realism, close attention must be paid to American attitudes toward marriage through discussions of race, class, and gender at the turn-of-the-century. Attitudes toward marriage express important cultural values, beliefs, and ideas about a great number of things besides marriage. By opening up textual conversations between *Megda* (1891) and *The Awakening* (1899), *An Imperative Duty* (1891) and *Iola Leroy* (1892), and *Contending Forces* (1900) and *The House of Mirth* (1905), this study attempts to prove that marriage is used as a forum for discussing race, class, and gender politics during the Age of Realism. Marriage becomes a source for imagining and interrogating the possibilities of harmonious communities based upon race, gender, and class equality. On an American scene largely characterized by moral decline, fiction writings of the realist era developed a discourse of modern marriage.

Though different, Chopin, Harper, Howells, Kelley, and Wharton are linked to a common literary outlook, realism, in their depictions of marriage. Marriage is both a significant institution and social relationship. I have chosen these six authors because of their detailed and extensive presentations of marriage within the idiom of realism. Kelley, Harper, and Hopkins's works affirm marriage, while Chopin, Howells, and Wharton's works express suspicion about marriage and its potential consequences. All six novels question the extent to which marriage in an imperfect society will allow their protagonists to assert themselves and develop as individual women. *American Realist Fictions of Marriage* contributes to an on-going debate that is more about realism's all-too-tidy focus on canonical writers Kate Chopin, William Dean Howells, and Edith Wharton by investigating the particular kinds of contributions writers less traditionally included in the realist canon, Emma Kelley, Frances Harper, and Pauline Hopkins, made to intellectual thought on matrimony. I hope that *American Realist Fictions of Marriage* will contribute to a reconsideration of how we read realism by erasing the boundaries, which impose limitations on dialogues between these authors and their texts.

The marriage fiction of Kate Chopin, Frances Harper, Pauline Hopkins, William Dean Howells, Emma Kelley, and Edith Wharton defines marriage as a partnership toward social progress. Their novels evaluate the extent to which marriage either preserves or pulls down the social order. At the center of each novel is the question of whether or not its protagonist has the moral fiber and social skills to not only establish but also maintain successful intimate social relationships. The possibility or impossibility of marriage for the protagonist functions as a larger metaphor for the probability and improbability of proposed unions between black and white, men and women, and equality among social classes. Marriage, ultimately, is presented as a viable solution for racism, sexism, and class difference.

American Realist Fictions of Marriage proposes that these six novelists appropriated realist techniques to express their anxieties about the unpredictability of middle-class life. Their works consider the problem of the "color line," sexism, and class boundaries. For this reason, we find many negative and stereotyped references to them in realist novels.[47] Questions considered in the novels and explored in *American Realist Fictions of Marriage* include: What is marriage? Who can enter the marriage contract? What are the central reasons for marriage? Do men and women have fairness and flexibility in marriage? Does society set the terms of a marriage? What obligations and rights are involved in the marital contract? What do the women characters in these novels suggest about fiction's impact on attitudes toward the representations of women and marriage? *American Realist Fictions of Marriage* explores these questions by reexamining realism's relation to the material realities of the social world through marriage and its fictive constructions of race, gender, and class. Kate Chopin, Frances Harper, Pauline Hopkins, William Dean Howells, Emma Kelley, and Edith Wharton wrote their novels at a time when social distinctions of gender, race, and class were changing. Through an examination of their inter-textual dialogues, I map the role that realism plays in seldom explored textual conversations about marriage between these writers during the Age of Realism.

Traditional views of marriage in the United States have roots in Christian religious views and church law. "Traditionalists considered marriage a special contract whose vows involved much more than a horizontal exchange between two people. It also involved the promise each party made vertically to God."[48] Marriage was first and foremost a covenant with God. In *Love American Style: Divorce and the American Novel,* Kimberly Freeman gives a historical account of marriage in American culture. Changing requirements of marriage in the eighteenth and nineteenth-centuries placed an increased emphasis on love and emotion as primary sources of marital satisfaction.[49] In Puritan cultural traditions as early as the 1600s, marriage was viewed as a contract. Though love was not necessarily part of that marital contract, there was the possibility that it could develop during the marriage. By the eighteenth and nineteenth-centuries, views of marriage began to change, and love became an integral part of the marriage contract. Freeman writes, "Underlying the rising importance of love in marriage was the implication of a sense of individual fulfillment from love and from marriage."[50] Marriage became such a desired marker of social identification that it began to parallel the desire for accumulation of wealth, a requirement of consumer culture. Freeman argues, "The desire for the ideal husband or wife parallels the consumer desire for new products, a desire that is inherently unquenchable. The ideal marriage becomes another commodity in the manufacturing of the American Dream."[51]

Morality is at the center of both marriage and realism's ideologies. "The Dean of American Letters" maintained a philosophy of realism's moral economy and the realist writer's responsibility to abide by economy and not excess. For Howells, a novelist has a moral responsibility to "revise fixed notions about the nature of what is real."[52] Howells imposes a moral order on the realist world he envisions, and marriage is the quintessential institution, which can strengthen the social fabric. Yet divorce threatens that social stability. Brook Thomas argues, "Society depends on the sense of duty and obligation most fully developed in individuals tested by institutions like marriage."[53] Wai-Chee Dimock has argued, "If we might speak of the 'cultural work' of the realistic novel, a crucial part of that work is surely to educate our moral sensibility, to instill in us a capacity for outrage as well as a capacity for acquiescence"[54] Thereby, authorial depictions of marriage in realist fiction offer models for developing moral character, commitment, and social responsibility.

Both the institution of marriage and marriage plots of realist novels are concerned with the extent to which a husband and wife embrace moral responsibility, compromise, and exercise free will. A closer look at male and female roles in marriage indicates that marriage was based on hierarchical relationships where the husband and wife have complementary roles. The husband is always the head of the family even though Christian theology stipulates that husband and wife are "one flesh."[55] Kimberly Freeman asserts, "Matrimony can be of inestimable worth to society in that by providing a man and woman with the comforts of a relationship built on quiet affection and civility it educates them to an awareness of their responsibilities to men and women at large"[56] Either a preserver or destroyer of social order, marriage functions as a metaphor for human and social imperfection.

The popularity of marriage as a topic during the nineteenth century is due to the fact that marriage is an integral part of the history and development of the plot and form of the novel genre. Marriage fiction looks at husband and wives' roles in their marriages and in society. "Husband and wife, each incomplete in themselves, were thought to complete each other."[57] Traditionally, husbands represented their wives in all legal and financial matters, omitting the possibility of women's authority and independence with regard to public and private business affairs. Depicted as an important kind of female identity and status in realist novels, marriage is also a marker of a woman's legal status. The ways in which marriage is written about during the late-nineteenth and early-twentieth-centuries suggests that marriage is the "real" preoccupation of American life and culture.

Allen F. Stein's *After the Marriage Vows: Marriage in American Literary Realism* discusses why certain writers during the realist period shared a mutual interest in marriage as a topic. Stein's study contains a selective literature review that examines the marriage plot in selected realist fiction. He compares the specific features of realism through the diverse marriage fiction of William Dean Howells, Henry James, Kate Chopin, Edith Wharton, and Robert Herrick. In his consideration of the varied nature of realism, Stein examines the plural presentations and responses each author's work has to marriage. He finds there to be a common pessimistic view of marriage among these authors. This strangeness of the marital relation and pessimism toward marriage is echoed in Nancy Cott's comparison of marriage to "the sphinx—a conspicuous and recognizable monument on the landscape, full of secrets" in the opening lines of her work *Public Vows: A History of Marriage and the Nation.*[58]

In her assessment of the "wonders or terrors" of matrimony, Cott argues that marriage is not the private matter that many people view it to be.[59] On the contrary, marriage is a very public matter. The institution of marriage itself does not have its basis in private life but public order instead. Cott writes, "Marital status is just as important to one's standing in the community and state as it is to self-understanding."[60] What may be considered a private marriage is actually a public model for the perpetuation and containment of social order on both a communal and larger national level. Cott's work is certainly in conversation with Peter Wallenstein's *Tell the Court I Love My Wife: Race, Marriage, and Law—An American History*, which explores the intersections between "race and sex, law and culture, marriage and property, identity and power."[61] Wallenstein's work argues that private relationships influenced public policy, and the public sphere governed individual personal lives. Wallenstein weaves together various studies surrounding court cases that demonstrate the impact of race on laws of marriage and the impact of marriage on laws of race. Although the United States lacked a national law of marriage, miscegenation laws discouraged interracial marriage by placing racial restrictions on matrimony.[62]

Lenore Weitzman's critical work *The Marriage Contract: Spouses, Lovers, and the Law* examines the impact law has upon the institution of marriage. He argues that every marriage is governed by the law of an unwritten contract. "Clearly, this marriage contract is unlike most contracts: its provisions are unwritten, its penalties are unspecified, and the terms of the contract are typically unknown to the contradicting parties."[63] Weitzman's study points out the insufficiency of the marriage contract, which has resulted in the shift of marriage from "a status to a status-contract."[64] (xix). Weitzman describes a shifting nineteenth-century world in which husband and wife neither possess the traditional privileges of status nor freedom that the marriage contract formerly provided. Hendrik Hartog explicitly argues that separation was "the practice through which nineteenth-century marital rights came into being."[65] In *Man and Wife in America: A History*, Hartog considers the legal culture of American marriage between 1790 and 1950 to examine marital life and marital identity for husbands and wives on the verge of separation. Hartog's critical study offers very important historical proof of what it meant to be married in a distinctly American legal culture that promoted marriage as "a permanent hierarchical relationship" from which there were no "possibilities for escape from that permanent relationship."[66]

In its exploration of law's conceptualization and regulation of marriage, Milton Regan's work asserts that the debate needs to address "the questions of how to accommodate individuality within community."[67] *Alone Together: Law and the Meanings of Marriage* describes the double identity of marriage, defined as the internal and external obligations spouses have to a marriage. Regan asserts, "Modern American attitudes toward marriage reflect two competing commitments: that spouses are separate individuals with their own distinct interests, and that they are members of a community who have special obligations to promote its welfare."[68] Randall Kennedy's *Interracial Intimacies: Sex, Marriage, Identity, and Adoption* looks at the influence modern American attitudes has toward interracial relationships. Kennedy's comprehensive critical study places itself in the middle of the debate of whether or not race is "a legitimate criterion for choosing a partner for romance or marriage."[69] His work considers the beliefs, cultural practices, laws, and socio-political institutions that have affected race relations in the most private spheres of American life across history. Ultimately, Kennedy argues that interracial intimacy is the glue that binds "American multiracial democracy."[70]

Perhaps visions of multiracial democracy through marriage are too idealistic. Stephanie Coontz's *Marriage, a History: How Love Conquered Marriage* describes marriage as a peculiar institution that we have had romanticized and placed misguided perceptions upon across history. She explains the American cultural fascination with the idea of marrying and its basis in a false precept of "some Golden Age of Marriage in the past."[71] Coontz's critical work succeeds in "debunking the idea that marriage was undergoing an unprecedented crisis" to show that "the institution of marriage has always been in flux."[72] She describes the ancient history of marriage and its strict basis in economics and politics. Coontz evaluates the changes in ideas and behaviors of marriage in the late eighteenth century where "people began to adopt the radical new idea that love should be the most fundamental reason for marriage."[73] Coontz argues that "the sentimentalization of the love-based marriage" in the late eighteenth through the twentieth centuries caused a crisis, which put the institution of marriage in jeopardy.[74]

Marriage, the common thread linking Chopin, Harper, Hopkins, Howells, Kelley, and Wharton, is the highest legal, social contract of moral commitment between two individuals. A popular subject matter during the nineteenth century in general, marriage is a vehicle for exploring both the problem of the "color line" and sexism that many women faced as they struggled to conform to or ignore society's expectations of them as wives and mothers. Moral decisions and ethical choices protagonists make about marriage espouse the possibility for either a racial or gender utopia, while simultaneously exposing the impossibility of these visions of harmony and egalitarianism.

Marriage becomes a symbol for proposed unions between blacks, whose marriages went unrecognized before emancipation. It also functions as a symbol of interracial union between black and white. Marriage also function as a metaphorical representation for the union of men and women of varying social class status. The impossibility of those expressed visions of racial equality and egalitarianism between the sexes, races, and classes is evident as well. In *The Ethnography of Manners,* Nancy Bentley argues, "The 'problem of American marriages' is the confusion of sexual and economic relations that undergirds American society."[75] Marriage functions as a representation for the problem of sexism in a society, which promotes sexist gender roles and values, and gender, becomes a more concrete category of representation or identification than race. Marriage provides an agency for women to socially circulate. A female industry of sorts, the "marriage market" parallels the expansion characterizing the scope of consumer capitalism in society.[76] Marriage also provides a forum for women to gain social power from their gender. Nancy Bentley argues that even in the event of a marriage's dissolution, "a suspiciously commercial circulation of women made possible by divorces and remarriage" exists.[77]

The chapters of *American Realist Fictions of Marriage* have been formulated to emphasize realist discussions of marriage that overlap in theme and style by comparison and contrast of writers and their various politics of genre. Moreover, the chapters in *American Realist Fictions of Marriage* have been crafted and organized to show the progression of realist attitudes toward marriage. The six novels I have chosen for this study are both peculiar to and representative of a larger trend. Chapter 1 is entitled "Conversion, Marriage, and Realism in Emma Kelley's *Megda* and Kate Chopin's *The Awakening*." Marriage is defined as a religious rite in Emma Kelley's *Megda*. However, Kate Chopin's *The Awakening* suggests that the institution of marriage may temporarily lead a husband and wife to a life of civility but ultimately results in the wife challenging social norms. Taken together, these two novels look at marriage as a forum for preserving both the religious and social order at the expense of patriarchy's influence and control over women's lives.

Chapter 2 is entitled "Marriage on the 'Color Line' in Frances Harper's *Iola Leroy* and William Dean Howells's *An Imperative Duty*." Marital love is characterized as duty to the racial uplift cause which two individuals share in Frances Harper's *Iola Leroy*. William Dean Howells's *An Imperative Duty* defines marriage as social progress toward racial equality. These two novels consider how the "color line" enforces racist notions of who is fit to marry who. Chapter 3 is entitled "Realism, Romance, and Questions of Marital Eligibility in Pauline Hopkins's *Contending Forces* and Edith Wharton's *The House of Mirth*." Pauline Hopkins's *Contending Forces* defines marriage based on the compensations that it can offer: loyalty to family, a rightful place in the community, virtue, and sanctioned passion and desire. Wharton's *The House of Mirth* suggests that there is no happiness for a woman outside of marriage because it affords women power, security, and social status. Both novels describe marriage as a woman's vocation, for it is her job to choose a suitable marriage partner so that she may marry and live well.

Chapter 1 uses the examples of Emma Kelley's *Megda* published in 1891 and Kate Chopin's *The Awakening* published in 1899 to explore how writers depicted marriage as able to social order, while acknowledging that even well-intentioned marital love can be destructive if blinded by the cultural prejudice of sexism. Both novels express concern about the influence of patriarchy on women's lives. Kelley and Chopin use realism to explore their heroines' relationships to social worlds and the conflicts therein. Kelley argues that women can find comfort and even maintain their own individual identities within marriage despite society's promotion of sexist values and traditional gender roles. Chopin argues that for better or worse, women's individual needs will assert themselves in a marriage. Both novelists suggest women's identities as wives and mothers are imposed gender roles placed upon women.

Kate Chopin's *The Awakening* is a novel of manners with strong elements of realism. It outright rejects the definition of marriage as happiness and fulfillment for women. Chopin attacks marriage, "which by its very nature does not place individual fulfillment above ties to others."[78] Marriage is simply another form of oppression perpetuated upon women that results in a further divide between the sexes. Chopin highlights the gender inequality and resulting consequences of the alleged "storybook" marriage, where the supposedly perfectly matched husband and wife live harmoniously and happily-ever-after.

Chopin overtly links marriage to a society based on social contract. The Pontellier marriage is observed by a society, which seeks to determine whether the parties involved are observing the manners and customs required of them as husband, wife, and productive citizens of society. This is an example of the private sphere of marriage in a very public domain. Chopin succeeds at "devaluating marriage as character-shaping and society-sustaining institution."[79] Chopin presents the inevitability of marriage stifling the feminine identity of her protagonist Edna. Edna is not a submissive woman, so she rebels against the demands married life places upon her. *The Awakening* focuses on the suffering and pain within a marriage in a society that commodifies and prevents women from liberating themselves. It is clear that Chopin considers marriage "valid only insofar as it allows individuals to attain self-fulfillment."[80] Edna is neither able to maintain a fulfilling life nor find an authentic identity as a married woman. Yet Emma Kelley's Meg accepts the submission that marriage requires.

In *Megda,* Emma Kelley appears to promote the idea that a marriage results in happiness and fulfillment for a woman. Marriage becomes "'a wonderful and powerful agent in the development and formation of a woman's character'" in *Megda*.[81] Marriage becomes necessary for Meg to realize her worth and embrace a well-rounded identity. She can only fulfill the demands of her womanly nature within her marriage. Meg only comes to this realization after unsuccessfully resisting submission to God's spiritual calling upon her life. Because marriage is a sacred rite, Meg realizes that submission and not rebellion is required within the socio-religious institution of marriage. A woman does not become a truly fulfilled woman until she is married, just as a sinner cannot become a saint until there has been repentance and acceptance of salvation.

The fact that Kelley links marriage with religion supports her belief that marriage is not a social contract but a religious rite of passage. Meg simultaneously struggles to convert to Christianity and to marry. Allen Stein asserts, "Marriage, particularly for a woman, involves a certain amount of submission."[82] Once she submits to the Christian faith, the pathway toward marriage is made clear. Kelley's *Megda* demonstrates that marriage can preserve the religious social order. Men and women can find comfort in marriage and still maintain appropriate patterns of social behavior. In the case of Meg and Reverend Stanley's marriage, there is a preservation of the social order but a revision of the pattern of behavior. Meg is not a weak, submissive wife to a controlling husband. Meg and Rev. Stanley's partnership is based on camaraderie and friendship. "Marriage is the only equation where two halves do not make a whole. It requires two wholes."[83] Within their marriage, Meg and Rev. Stanley place emphasis on the preservation of each of their individual spirits and different identities in order for the marital union to work.

Shifting to marriage as duty to the race cause and social progress, Chapter 2 demonstrates the importance of marriage to "race" fiction of the nineteenth century. Frances Harper and William Dean Howells use the highest moral act of commitment between two individuals, marriage, as the stage upon which to play their differing political commentary on the problem of the "color line." Both Harper and Howells use their characters' moral decisions and ethical choices surrounding marriage as realist narrative strategy to espouse the possibility for a racial utopia. Simultaneously, these two authors expose the impossibility of that vision of equality and egalitarianism. Literal marriages take place in both novels, but marriage also functions as the central metaphor for Harper and Howells's interrogation of proposed unions between opposites or dichotomies in the social and political realms.

Both novelists consider the possibilities and social consequences of the marriage of North and South (Reconstruction) as well the marriage between a black and a white individual.[84] The "color line" was a representation for the boundaries between polar opposites that was to prevent "marriages" of this sort. The "color line" enforces racist notions of who is fit to marry who. Both Iola and Rhoda have unknowingly passed for white. The two protagonists' reactions and responses to finding out their true mulatto racial identities differ. Rhoda chooses to identify with her white heritage and decides to pass for the remainder of her life. She marries the white Dr. Olney. Her true mulatto racial identity becomes their private secret because she does not physically appear to have black blood within her. Rhoda and Olney's interracial marriage can only flourish abroad in Europe, for it is neither socially sanctioned nor accepted on American soil. Howells attempts to depict their marriage as reconciliation between the races to represent of the healing that mixed-race marriages can bring to the American consciousness. Howells believes these "marriages" can restore social order and raise the morale of the nation.

In *After the Vows Were Spoken*, Allen Stein argues that Howells's marriage fiction maintains "an essentially sentimental perspective of marriage."[85] In order for the happily-ever-after ending to occur, Howells must place Rhoda and Olney's marital union in a foreign context where it can be legally sanctioned. Unlike Rhoda, Frances Harper's Iola quickly aligns herself with her black heritage. Iola chooses to ignore her white heritage, and she marries a black man of her same social and cultural standing. Yet Hazel Carby argues that "marriage was not presented by Harper as the culmination and raison d'etre of a woman's being."[86] Iola and Dr. Latimer's marriage "fashions for the fortunate couple a little sphere of civility and order in a world that otherwise is often chaotic and threatening."[87] "Love constructed as duty was the ideal mode of courtship and marriage during the mid-nineteenth century."[88] Iola's marriage is socially sanctioned and accepted, for she joins her husband in the racial uplift cause. Their marriage has its basis in social work instead of love or passion.

Chapter 3 presents a comparative study of two largely unpaired novels, *Contending Forces* (1900) and *The House of Mirth* (1905). These two novels define marriage as a woman's profession. Marriage becomes a woman's life's work. Her sole job is to choose an honorable marriage partner. Women who were meant to become beautiful objects had as their only responsibility to embody beauty. As supreme and artistic perfections, these women had as their job to marry well. Edith Wharton's *The House of Mirth* and Pauline Hopkins' *Contending Forces* describe the particular and unconscionable prescribed relationship single women aspiring to marry had to beauty. Both novels reveal how beauty is duped.

In *Contending Forces*, fairytale love and the "storybook" marriage are attainable for the physically beautiful mulatto character Sappho despite assaults upon her virtue and threatened exposure of her troubled past. Whether Sappho marries becomes a predictor of whether or not she will survive the cruelties society can perpetuate on not just black women but mixed-race women. Sappho Clark is an extremely beautiful mulatto woman whose aura captivates men. Motivated by socioeconomic status, beauty functions as both social capital and commodity according to the culture and taste which dictate society's capacity to appreciate and exploit her beauty.

In *The House of Mirth,* Edith Wharton demonstrates how race and gender—two social constructs—are related by showing that gender is a more concrete category than race. The notion of perfect happiness in marriage is unattainable despite the protagonist Lily's beauty. "Little as there is in the depiction of marriage in *The House of Mirth* that seems to recommend the institution to anyone not seeking power in the polite New York society at the turn of the twentieth century, the novel does not condemn marriage."[89] Marriage offers both power and security in Lily's society. As a married woman, Lily can do those things, which lead to her destruction as an unmarried woman. Edith Wharton, "records the rise and fall of Lily's social position as dictated by the unstable currency of gossip."[90] Marriage becomes the metaphor for social progress in *The House of Mirth*. For it at the expense of beauty that Lily and Sappho are duped by society's forced expectations upon them as women who must marry.

A central question posed across these three chapters is whether marriage will allow each female protagonist to have autonomy within the marriage contract. Choices made by the female protagonists about whether to marry at all, who to marry, or whether to separate from a marriage metaphorically express the possibilities of racial and gender equality, simultaneously revealing threats to those visions for society. *American Realist Fictions of Marriage* argues that some American realist novels use marriage as a forum for imagining and interrogating the possibilities of harmonious societies of racial and gender equality. The manner in which marriage, a commercial and social relation, is written about during this period suggests that marriage is a preoccupation of American culture. Kate Chopin, Frances Harper, Pauline Hopkins, William Dean Howells, Emma Kelley, and Edith Wharton use marriage to explore the problems of the "color line," sexism, and class that highlighted categories of difference and social boundaries. Ultimately, what these novelists' works reveal is that gender is a more concrete category of representation or identification than race. *Megda, Iola Leroy, An Imperative Duty, The Awakening, Contending Forces,* and *The House of Mirth* pose uncomfortable questions about social justice, class-standing, and race and gender equality that lie at the center of our national experience.

Realism functions as a mode of narration for fictive constructions of marriage and the race, class, and gender upheavals these depictions of marriage represent. Many realist novels got their structure from the marriage plot, and *American Realist Fictions of Marriage* studies the marriage plot in the context of shifting gender roles during the late-nineteenth and early twentieth-centuries. The novels selected for this study conform to marriage plot structure, and they contribute to intellectual exchanges on companionate marriage where gender equality is at the core of discourses on modern marriage.

Just as "race" is crucial to our understanding of realism, so are gender politics. Key theoretical approaches to race and gender have also enhanced my investigation of these six authors' high regard for or misgivings about American marriage as depicted by the range of marital behavior exhibited by the characters in their novels. In *Reconstructing Womanhood,* Hazel Carby's argument that "we need more feminist work that interrogates sexual ideologies for their racial specificity and acknowledges whiteness, not just blackness, as a racial categorization" suggests that race and gender politics are inseparable.[91] bell hooks takes the argument a step further in her assertion that intersections between race, gender, and class are systems of oppression in patriarchy that devalue and marginalize black women.[92] Gender theorists such as Judith Butler and Kate Bornstein have argued that gender is socially constructed. Both these critical works argue that gender is performed. Butler and Bornstein also conclude that gender is a socialization process that is ongoing. As a result, characteristics of masculinity and femininity are learned but innately predetermined. These studies explore the extent to which culture stimulates shifts in society's expectations and requirements that govern gender and determine delineations of masculinity and femininity.

Howellsian realism was in large part related to the intense gender anxieties regarding the profession of authorship. Women writers have long "exposed the masculinist causes of social and legal inequities and proposed alternative social roles acknowledging the interests and importance of women."[93] Five of the authors incorporated within *American Realist Fictions of Marriage* are women, and the theoretical exploration of the relationship between gender and realism in Barbara Hochman's *Getting at the Author: Reimagining Books and Reading in the Age of Realism* has been instrumental in my approach to women writing realism. Hochman writes about the self-reflexivity of women writers who were highly self-conscious of themselves as "women on stage" producing literature in a consumerist market system of production and exchange.[94] Hochman argues, "Thus the woman onstage exaggerated and epitomized certain features of women's existence in general. But the situation of the actress simultaneously reflected many aspects of an author's position in relation to the turn-of-century readership."[95] The "woman on stage" is a metaphor for women writers at the turn-of-the-century who find themselves and their works under criticism. Nancy Glazener supports Hochman's assertion about authorial self-consciousness about writing and audiences reading realism. Glazener argues that "public conversations about genre did not merely affect texts after their composition, but also affected authors' addresses to their readers and even their understandings of their own activities."[96] As performers on stage, women writers are self-conscious of the way they represent themselves and their work for public audiences. Hochman associates the vulnerability on the "woman on stage" with reading and writing women's fiction at the turn-of-the-century.

Elsa Nettels's critical work shifts the discussion from women writing publicly to a discussion of the appropriate language or discourse for women's novels. Nettels points to the complication of having a gendered discourse when language is already patriarchal-centered. In *Language and Gender in American Fiction*, she considers "the illusion that polarities such as *masculine* and *feminine* signify the balance of equals."[97]

Nettels's work has been particularly useful to my discussion of gender as a social construction in chapter one's discussion of the influence of patriarchal authority and sexist gender roles in Emma Kelley and Kate Chopin's novels. Nettels finds that the relationship between language and gender is one that promotes polarity and binary opposition. Nettels points out the power two culturally biased and charged words, "masculine" and "feminine." These two words have determined constructions of gender that result in inequality, differentiation between the language of men and women, and sexist discourses.

Works such as Ann duCille's *The Coupling Convention: Sex, Text, and Tradition in Black Women's Fiction* demonstrate the currency that distinctly black marriage plots possess in their critiques of both gender and racial issues.[98] duCille argues that African American novelists of the nineteenth- and early-twentieth-centuries developed their own conventional marriage plot which is distinctly different and separate from the white middle class marriage plot typically found in mainstream American literature. duCille labels the distinctly African American marriage plot "the coupling convention" of African American novels, but traces the development of the convention through African American women's novels specifically.[99] duCille's detailed examination of "the coupling convention" in Nella Larsen's *Quicksand* (1928), Zora Neale Hurston's *Their Eyes Were Watching God* (1937) and *Seraph on the Suwanee* (1948), and Jessie Fauset's *Plum Bun* (1929) places these works in conversation with other mainstream "white" novels of the twentieth century to show that both marginalized and canonical works have influenced one another's marriage plots.

While duCille seeks to delete notions of essentialism, tradition, and canons that promote one master narrative regarding marriage plots in fiction, I extend her argument further to say the marriage plot has been specifically used by African American women writers Frances Harper and Pauline Hopkins as a meta-literary convention. The marriage plots in *Iola Leroy* and *Contending Forces* function as commentary on sentimental, romance, historical, and realist conventions within the plots of their novels. These two African-American women writers use the marriage plot to point out the uses of multiple genres and shortcomings of individual genres. Slippage between genres in *Iola Leroy* and *Contending Forces* is a reflection of various historical ambiguities about race, class, and gender during the time period. Cross-fertilization is a theme in these two novels, which incorporate conventions of multiple genres to create their discourses on modern marriage.[100]

In *Domestic Allegories of Political Desire: The Black Heroine's Text at the Turn of the Century*, Claudia Tate turns her attention to the variety of marriage plots and specific features of those plots that African-American women writers depicted in their romance and sentimental narratives. One common feature that Tate finds within these varied marriage plots is idealized depictions of marriage or "domestic allegories of political desire."[101] Tate's work explores why the marriage plot is useful and what the marriage plot conveys in African-American women's texts. Tate claims that African-American women adopt the marriage plot convention from the specific genres of the sentimental novel and the romance. They do not create their own distinct convention as duCille's work suggests. Instead, African-American women adopt the convention as a feature of the genre. However, in their appropriation of the convention as part of the novel form, these women use marriage as a literal representation of liberation to present arguments for social reform, equality, and civil liberty in their fictional representations. My work looks at how the writers I have selected use marriage to evaluate the possibility of racial and gender equality and social progress. From this perspective, marriage affects the partners involved in the marriage, and the success or failure of the marriage also affects society at large.

As a study of literary responses to or interpretations of marriage, *American Realist Fictions of Marriage* examines the literary works of Chopin, Harper, Hopkins, Howells, Kelley, and Wharton to consider the literary historical significance of American debates about marriage. *American Realist Fictions of Marriage* also considers the implication of the role marriage has in shaping the female self. Furthermore, this dissertation examines how, for the six writers I have selected, marriage is the foundation of society, which can protect against society's ills. The function of marriage in society as expressed through these six novels reveals that the concept of love is largely a social construction. *American*

Realist Fictions of Marriage considers the complex ways that beliefs and policies regarding marriage have affected national understandings of gender roles, racial difference, class, and citizenship. Ultimately, I hope *American Realist Fictions of Marriage* will contribute to scholarship on the discourse of modern marriage to show that marriage was not just a private relationship but part of the wider social structure. *American Realist Fictions of Marriage* stresses that the underlying American discourse on gender and marriage reflected a shifting balance of public visibility and power toward women.

Notes

1. During the period 1890–1899, the decade commonly referred to as the "racial 1890s," race and gender tensions climaxed to an all-time high. Shirley Logan, *We Are Coming: The Persuasive Discourse of Nineteenth-Century Black Women* (Carbondale: Southern Illinois University Press, 1999) describes the post-Reconstruction Era as a period where "white supremacy in the South and general black oppression were consolidated" (xi).
2. Daniel Borus, *Writing Realism: Howells, James, and Norris in the Mass Market* (Chapel Hill: University of North Carolina Press, 1989), 4.
3. *Ibid.*, 17.
4. Kathleen Pfeiffer, *Race Passing and American Individualism* (Amherst: University of Massachusetts Press, 2003), 40.
5. Hildegard Hoeller, *Edith Wharton's Dialogue with Realism and Sentimental Fiction* (Gainesville: University Press of Florida, 2000), 13.
6. William Dean Howells, "Editor's Study," *Harper's New Monthly Magazine*. November (1889): 966.
7. Borus, 14.
8. *Ibid.*
9. *Ibid.*, 99.
10. Gene Andrew Jarrett, *Deans and Truants: Race and Realism in African American Literature* (Philadelphia: University of Pennsylvania Press, 2007), 44.
11. Brook Thomas, *American Literary Realism and the Failed Promise of Contract* (Berkeley: University of California Press, 1997), 38.
12. Eric J. Sundquist, *American Realism: New Essays* (Boston: Johns Hopkins University Press, 1982), vii.
13. *Webster's II New Riverside Dictionary* (Boston: Houghton Mifflin, 1996), 569.

14. Walter Benn Michaels, *The Gold Standard and the Logic of Capitalism: American Literature at the Turn of the Century* (Berkeley: University of California Press, 1987), 36.
15. Nancy Bentley, *The Ethnography of Manners: Hawthorne, James, Wharton* (Cambridge: Cambridge University Press, 1995), 2.
16. *Ibid.*, 2–3.
17. See Elizabeth Ammons's article "Expanding the Canon of American Realism," *Documents of American Realism and Naturalism*, Ed. Donald Pizer (Carbondale: Southern Illinois University Press, 1988), 435–452. This article has a full discussion of canonicity issues as related to American literary realism. Ammons has a multicultural vision of American literary realism, and she offers pedagogical approaches to teaching realism that recognize this marginalized diversity in both writers and intellectual thought during the time period. Ammons expresses the need for contemporary scholarship on realism that takes into account racial and cultural differences among writers during the Age of Realism.
18. René Wellek, *Concepts of Criticism* (New Haven: Yale University Press, 1963), 240–241.
19. Alfred Habegger, "Realism," *Documents of American Realism and Naturalism*, Ed. Donald Pizer (Carbondale: Southern Illinois University Press, 1988), 355–356.
20. Warner Berthoff, *The Ferment of Realism: American Literature, 1884–1919* (Cambridge: Cambridge University Press, 1981), 1.
21. Borus, 4.
22. Habegger, 361.
23. Stanley Corkin, *Realism and the Birth of the Modern United States* (Athens: University of Georgia, 1996), 1.
24. Michele Birnbaum, *Race, Work, and Desire in American Literature, 1860–1930* (Cambridge: Cambridge University Press, 2003), 21.
25. Michaels, 27.
26. *Ibid.*
27. Amy Kaplan, *The Social Construction of American Realism* (Chicago: University of Chicago Press, 1988), 9.
28. June Howard, *Form and History in American Literary Naturalism* (Chapel Hill: University of North Carolina Press, 1985), 70.
29. Naturalism is both a genre of writing and a literary movement. Often talked about in tandem with realism, naturalist works carefully consider how the forces of nature, society, environment, and heredity impact characters' lives. While these characters in naturalist novels attempt to exercise free will, their attempts are useless. Despite their choices, circumstances beyond characters' control seal their fates. Free will is, ultimately, an illusion at best. Naturalist novels typically focus on lower class characters, and they employ social Darwinist rhetoric. Some writers associated with naturalism include but are not limited to the following writers: Stephen Crane, Theodore Dreiser, Ellen Glasgow, Jack London, Frank Norris, John Steinbeck, Edith Wharton, and Richard Wright.

30. Michael Davitt Bell, *The Problem of American Realism: Studies in the Cultural History of a Literary Idea* (Chicago: University of Chicago Press, 1993), 8–9.
31. Lois A. Cuddy, and Claire M. Roche, *Evolution and Eugenics in American Literature and Culture, 1880–1940* (Lewisburg: Bucknell University Press, 2003), 22.
32. Borus, 4.
33. Amy Kaplan, "Realism and Absent Things in American Life," *Documents of American Realism and Naturalism*, Ed. Donald Pizer (Carbondale: Southern Illinois University Press, 1998), 409.
34. Ammons, 436.
35. John Haller, *Outcasts from Evolution: Scientific Attitudes of Racial Inferiority, 1849–1900* (Urbana: University of Illinois Press, 1971), x.
36. George Frederickson, *The Black Image in the White Mind* (New York: Harper and Row, 1972), xii.
37. *Ibid.*, xiii.
38. Cathy Boeckmann, *A Question of Character: Scientific Racism and the Genres of American Fiction, 1892–1912* (Tuscaloosa: University of Alabama Press, 2000), 9.
39. Lee D. Baker, *From Savage to Negro: Anthropology and the Construction of Race, 1896–1954* (Berkeley: University of California Press, 1998), 1.
40. Kenneth Warren, *Black and White Strangers* (Chicago: University of Chicago Press, 1993), 10.
41. Rayford W. Logan coined the term "nadir." The post-Reconstruction Era, commonly referred to as the "nadir," or the lowest point in black history, is also a historical moment in which some of the most compelling intellectual and literary contributions articulating the progress and uplift of the black race were published. For a fuller discussion of the "nadir" and post-Reconstruction see Logan's book, *The Betrayal of the Negro from Rutherford B. Hayes to Woodrow Wilson* (New York: Collier, 1965).
42. Warren, 6.
43. While Lord Byron is credited as first inventing or using this expression in *Don Juan* (1833), Mark Twain is most well-known for the following statement: "Truth is stranger than fiction, but it is because Fiction is obliged to stick to possibilities; Truth isn't." I found this quote by Twain on the Brainy Quotes website http://www.brainyquotes.com/quotes/quotes/m/marktwain/22865.html. William Wells Brown also entitles a chapter in *Clotel* (1853) "Truth Stranger Than Fiction."
44. Wai-Chee Dimock, "The Economy of Pain: Capitalism, Humanitarianism, and the Realistic Novel," *Raritan: A Quarterly Review* 9.4 (1990), 9.
45. *Ibid.*, 9.
46. Toni Morrison, *Playing in the Dark: Whiteness and the Literary Imagination* (New York: Vintage, 1992), 6.

47. The "color line," a term loosely thrown around during the mid-to-late-nineteenth-century, referred to the line of distinction drawn between the black and white races. The "color line" represented an invisible boundary enforcing the strict separation of the races and the fear of white racial impurity as a result of miscegenation or mixed-race unions.
48. Thomas, 134.
49. Kimberly Freeman, *A Love American Style: Divorce and the American Novel, 1881–1976* (New York: Routledge, 2003), 12.
50. *Ibid.*, 13.
51. *Ibid.*, 13–14.
52. Thomas, 144.
53. Thomas, 135.
54. Dimock, 9.
55. See Genesis 2:24 in the *New International Version Student Bible*. Chapter two talks about the first marriage God ordained between Adam and Eve.
56. Freeman, 19.
57. *Ibid.*, 12.
58. Nancy F. Cott, *Public Vows: A History of Marriage and the Nation* (Cambridge: Harvard University Press, 2000), 1.
59. *Ibid.*
60. *Ibid.*
61. Peter Wallenstein, *Tell the Court I Love My Wife: Race, Marriage, and Law—An American History* (New York: Palgrave, 2002), 5.
62. *Ibid.*, 50, 56.
63. Lenore J. Weitzman, *The Marriage Contract: Spouses, Lovers, and the Law* (New York: The Free Press, 1981), xv.
64. *Ibid.*, xix.
65. Hendrik Hartog, *Man and Wife in America: A History* (Cambridge: Harvard University Press, 2000), 1.
66. *Ibid.*, 2.
67. Milton C. Regan, Jr., *Alone Together: Law and the Meanings of Marriage* (New York: Oxford University Press, 1999), 3.
68. *Ibid.*
69. Randall Kennedy, *Interracial Intimacies: Sex, Marriage, Identity, and Adoption* (New York: Pantheon, 2003), 33.
70. *Ibid.*, 39.
71. Stephanie Coontz, *Marriage, a History: How Love Conquered Marriage* (New York: Penguin, 2005), 1.
72. *Ibid.*
73. *Ibid.*, 5.
74. *Ibid.*

75. Bentley, 202.
76. Augusta Rohrbach, *Truth Stranger Than Fiction: Race, Realism, and the U.S. Literary Marketplace* (New York: Palgrave, 2002), 104.
77. Bentley, 163.
78. Allen F. Stein, *After the Vows Were Spoken: Marriage in American Literary Realism* (Columbus: Ohio State University Press, 1984), 165.
79. *Ibid.*, 166.
80. *Ibid.*, 176.
81. *Ibid.*, 181.
82. *Ibid.*, 176.
83. Johnny Parker, *Blueprints for Marriage: Building Love for a Lifetime* (Lanham, MD: PnumaLife Publishers, 2002), 5–6.
84. Reconstruction is generally defined as a period from approximately 1865–1877 in United States history characterized by the political resolve to address the social, cultural, and economic issues that surfaced with the readmission of the eleven Confederate states that had seceded from the Union at the time of the Civil War.
85. Stein, 50.
86. Hazel V. Carby, *Reconstructing Womanhood: The Emergence of the Afro-American Woman Novelist* (New York: Oxford University Press, 1987), 97.
87. Stein, 20.
88. Claudia Tate, *Domestic Allegories of Political Desire: The Black Heroine's Text at the Turn of the Century* (New York: Oxford University Press, 1992), 125.
89. Stein, 235.
90. Bentley, 190.
91. Carby, 18.
92. bell hooks uses unconventional lower case letters for the first letter of her first and last name. hooks suggests that she uses lower case letters to remove the focus from her name and to place proper emphasis on her actual texts.
93. Gene Andrew Jarett, *Deans and Truants: Race and Realism in African-American Literature* (Philadelphia: University of Pennsylvania Press, 2007), 25.
94. Barbara Hochman, *Getting at the Author: Reimagining Books and Reading in the Age of Realism* (Amherst: University of Massachusetts Press, 2001), 71.
95. *Ibid.*, 72.
96. Nancy Glazener, *Reading for Realism: The History of a U.S. Literary Institution, 1850–1910* (Durham: Duke University Press, 1997), 53.
97. Elsa Nettels, *Language, Race, and Social Class in Howells's America* (Lexington: University Press of Kentucky, 1988), 185.
98. The first letter of Anne duCille's last name is spelled with a lower-case letter and the third letter is capitalized. duCille is a French name, and this is reflected in the spelling.

99. Ann duCille, *The Coupling Convention: Sex, Text, and Tradition in Black Women's Fiction* (New York: Oxford University Press, 1993), 3–4.
100. See M. Giulia Fabi's article "Reconstructing the Race: The Novel After Slavery" in the *Cambridge Companion to The African American Novel.* Fabi uses the term "cross-fertilization" to describe the novel-writing practices of some African-American writers who blended conventions and features from various genres of writing in their novels written after slavery.
101. Tate, 1.

Chapter 1

Conversion, Marriage, and Realism in Emma Kelley's *Megda* and Kate Chopin's *The Awakening*

Social standards of marriage and the ranges of resulting marital behaviors among protagonists in Emma Dunham-Kelly's *Medgda* (1891) and Kate Chopin's *The Awakening* (1899) demonstrate both the enticing prospects and disdain for American marriage during the Age of Realism. Many realist writers felt that marriage's moral currency and political economy could restore morality to an American nation characterized by race and gender tensions, the evolution of capitalism, and industrialism and market exchange. Realism is a literature about social change, and marriage is an institution that has the power to change social relations and raise morale. These depictions of marriage not only illustrate the social changes taking place on an American scene, but they also reveal something of vital importance about realist writers and their outlooks on social relations. In most cases, marriage literally and metaphorically represented hierarchies between men and women, white and black, lower, middle, and upper class. Marriage holds a distinct place in the cultural imagination of writers who sought to look closely at the quintessential social relation, marriage, for answers about a world rapidly evolving socially, culturally, and politically.

Kate Chopin rejects sentimental and romantic definitions of marriage as happiness and fulfillment for women in her novel, *The Awakening*. This notion of the "storybook" marriage, where husband and wife life happily-ever-after, frames the gender equality implicit in this type of marriage which is based upon social contract. Marriage, a requirement of consumer culture, is ultimately what causes Edna's suffering. While marriage provides the benefits of wealth and class, the problems that occur in Edna's marriage far outweigh these consumer benefits. Edna struggles to confront issues of autonomy. Though married, Edna is alone. Through Edna's struggles to copes with the demands placed upon her by marriage, Kate Chopin gives a realist depiction of marriage and its functions "as an institution externally beneficial but internally fraught with misery and self-denial for women."[1] Chopin characterizes marriage as a system of domination and subordination. Marriage "harbored inequalities inconsistent with American principles of liberty and equality."[2] Marriage is an unequal relationship where a wife's role is to depend upon her husband. "The story that marriage was invented for the protection of women is still the most widespread myth about the origins of marriage."[3] Marriage becomes a forum for preserving the social order at the expense of patriarchy's influence and power over women's lives. Chopin argues that women's identity as wives and mothers are imposed gender roles placed upon them. Marital entrapment becomes a form of bondage that Edna must free herself from in *The Awakening*.

Despite the realism of Chopin's carefully crafted depictions of the failure of the marriage contract and its consequences, Edna's awakening and death are described in sentimental and romantic terms. The narrator's attitude towards Edna is one of sympathy and criticism, and the novel's theme of self-realization is a powerful romantic trope in the novel. Edna has a romantic vision for her life, but the novel also portrays the realist truth of the limits of both Edna's literal existence and dreams of emancipation. Edna possesses admirable romantic values, and we as readers are sympathetic to Edna's need for freedom and self-discovery. For this reason, the description of her suicide evokes out sympathy. Chopin depicts Edna as a helpless victim of society. Like the sentimental heroine, she has been relentlessly pursued by a value system that she does not fit within. As a result, the only way Edna can escape society's prescriptions and expectations for her life is through death. Despite our sympathies for Edna, the reality remains that "marriage has constructed and reinforced hierarchical relations between men and women" in *The Awakening*.[4] The failed Pontellier marriage becomes a larger metaphor for a definition of marriage as human tragedy.

Emma Dunham-Kelley's *Megda* idealizes holy wedlock. Marriage marks the pathway to religious sanctity and culminates into the successful contemplation of a spiritual journey. Kelley defines marriage as submission to patriarchal and religious authority. The novel's self-titled protagonist must relinquish her autonomous and selfish identity in order to convert to Christianity and receive the reward of marriage. The narrator repeatedly calls upon the reader to pity Meg's depraved condition. This sentimental technique also emphasizes the novel's realist investment in Meg's character interiority. As such, the novel vacillates back and forth with its employment of conventions of sentiment and realism. A clearly realist feature of the novel is the detailed character construction and character development of Meg. Emphasis is largely placed on Meg's character development, and less emphasis is placed upon the actual plot of the novel. The events of the novel are highly predictable. It is clear from the outset of the novel that Meg will marry and live happily-ever-after even though the novel extensively details her struggle to follow that pathway of repentance, conversion, and marriage.

Emma Dunham-Kelley's *Megda* focuses on the sanctity of marriage where "husband and wife become one flesh."[5] From this viewpoint, women need to be saved by God and by man. Marriage is a God-given right and sacrament. Marriage preserves both the religious and social order, and Meg makes the right ethical choices in the midst of her journey toward maturation and spiritual fulfillment. The romantic love between Meg and Reverend Stanley is realized through their faith in God. Kelley affirms a romantic view of marriage as a means to secular happiness and spiritual fulfillment for women. Marriage is a necessary step toward a woman's identity formation in the secular and sacred sense. Kelley promotes traditional roles of womanhood and conventional ideals of marriage. Marriage and religion combined ensure the sustenance of social order. By reinforcing traditional gender roles of men and women, Kelley asserts that the social order can in fact be preserved. The happily-ever-after can become a reality if religion maintains its proper place in society. Realistic and romantic ideas of marriage can share an equal existence in a world where morality is at the center of the valuation of marriage.

Writing during a decade when distinctions based on race, class, and especially gender were transitional, Emma Kelley's *Megda* and Kate Chopin's *The Awakening* express concerns about the influence of patriarchy upon women's lives. By paying particular attention to the institution of marriage and its public and private spheres of social influence, Kelley and Chopin consider relationships between women and the material realities by which they may be surrounded. Both novelists are critical of socially prescribed roles and duties for women, and they challenge gendered representations by male novelists. Marriage and the pursuit of it are central concerns in *Megda* and *The Awakening*, but unlike many novels of the realist era, marriage is not depicted as the ultimate source of happiness in these two novels. These two novels critique the lack of realism in usual portrayals of marriage as romantic and unproblematic. In *Megda* and *The Awakening* marriage is defined as an antagonistic force that works against a woman's autonomy. Edna's worldly marriage and Meg's spiritual marriage overturn the "storybook" marriage and present social definitions of marriage.

In tandem with realism's subscription to verisimilitude, Kelley and Chopin created believable fictions, and their memorable heroines' stories mirror the lives of ordinary women. The events that occur in the two novels are plausible instead of sensational or dramatic. Reality is presented in objective and comprehensive detail in both *Megda* and *The Awakening*. Character development is more important than the action or plot. Meg and Edna demonstrate that realist characters act on their own environments rather than simply reacting to them. Character is superior to circumstance in realist novels, and Meg and Edna appear in their real complexity of temperament, specifically in relation to their social class and identification as women.

Realism as a mode of representation for novels that centered around the topic of matrimony often offered ideal presentations of marriage. In realist novels written during 1870–1900, relationships between men and women were often a popular topic of discussion.[6] Questions of gender equality and sexism that were important to sustaining the social order were often at the center of some realist novels written during this period of intense racial paranoia. Marriage fiction during the realist era depicts wedlock as the symbolic culmination of racial, social, spiritual, and gender concerns women often faced. Patriarchal custom abhorred the idea that women existed as separate individuals with identities outside their relationships to others. Women often brought dowry or inherited wealth to a marriage, and they were expected to place their husband's needs above their own. Yet women belonged to their husbands, who had absolute control over the family. Husbands cared for and displayed their wives as ornaments, and women were often homemakers responsible for the domestic orders of the household. Women had a responsibility to educate and raise the children to become productive citizens of society.

"Gender," a term referring to the social characteristics associated with being male and female, is socially constructed. Attributes and relationships associated with being male or female are learned through a socialization process, and recognized differences between men and women are based upon assigned roles created and learned in families. Teresa Zackodnik argues, "Gender is repeatedly constituted by the performance of behaviors that we consider to be masculine or feminine."[7] The words "masculine" and "feminine" had extremely influential connotations. Masculine typically meant strong, dominant, or superior, while feminine meant weak, submissive, or inferior.[8] Gender analyses of these two charged words reveal how women's subordination is socially constructed. Because gender is part of the broader sociocultural context, Emma Kelley and Kate Chopin appear to confront realism for the social inequities that inscribe race, gender, and class differences in its discourse. Kelley's *Megda* and Chopin's *The Awakening* criticize concepts of gender that emphasize characteristics of men and women as delineations of masculinity and femininity.

Undoubtedly, realist novels played a role in the social construction of gender and sexuality. Some realist novels often explored expectations and values of men and women in various social settings. The relationship between realism and gender is difficult to characterize. Like race and class, gender is another category of difference used to promote inequality. Realism's intersection with questions of gender equality appears to hinge upon whether proposed differences between men and women are inherently biological or culturally ideological differences. These questions of behavioral traits and biological determinism echo the same questions that underlie popular racial-scientific thought of the time period. Like the term "race," the meaning of the term "gender" at the turn-of-the-century emerges within a context of consumer society characterized by exchange and production. Realist writers often depicted social worlds that encouraged "masks" of race and gender, pointing toward the performance aspects of the two social constructions.[9]

Kelley and Chopin reject the notion that women's subordination is biologically predetermined, and they promote the equal valuing of the similarities and differences between men and women and the roles they play in marriage. Both novelists indicate that a successful marriage benefits wife, husband, and society, pointing toward the positive influences of a "good" marriage versus the negative effects of a "bad" marriage. Even though Kelley and Chopin neither knew each other nor are they connected by race or class, their literary dialogue on gender links into a conversation. Their important contributions to realism criticize American systems, which isolate men and women in separate spheres and rigid marriage roles. However, at times Kelley and Chopin fall into the trap of voicing conventional assumptions about gender upon which a system of inequality is based.

The figure of the "woman onstage" is a metaphorical representation commonly found in realist texts.[10] This metaphor of the woman on stage can also be applied to the married woman. It explains the predicament of married women who find themselves on display for society's judgment of whether they have properly fulfilled their obligations as wife and mother. Edna and Meg are fictive constructions of literal women who find themselves on the stage of the "marriage market."[11] Even though marriage enables women to circulate socially and gain social power, the ideal marriage becomes a commodity in the American consumerist system. By profession, Kelley and Chopin are women writers on stage at the turn-of-the-century, and their two protagonists Meg and Edna are women characters on stage exemplary of real women.

Kate Chopin wrote prior to the "women's movement" of the twentieth century, but her novel *The Awakening* demonstrates the beginnings of the movement at the turn-of-the-century. *The Awakening,* a novel ahead of its time, encourages women to develop separate, independent identities despite society's demands for them to define themselves solely as wives and mothers. Chopin appears to suggest that if women want to be individuals, they must defy their marriage vows. A single lifestyle apart from marriage is the only source of identification that allows a woman to be herself. For Chopin, marriage does not provide currency for female self-identification. Instead, marriage consumes a woman's individual freedom. *The Awakening* is primarily a realist novel that focuses on Edna's moral dilemma to remain true to her marriage vows or fulfill her selfish desires. However, the genteel reading public and critics of the Gilded Age were grossly offended by *The Awakening*'s amoral depictions of white womanhood and the narrator's sympathy toward an immoral and condemned Edna.

Chopin's publication of *The Awakening* in 1899 led to scandal and the ending of her career. Yet it is of no surprise that *The Awakening* generated such scandal. Kate Chopin's Edna did not exemplify the values promoted by the cult of true womanhood.[12] Edna is anything but a "true woman" because she is sexually liberated. Yet decades after the scandal it caused, *The Awakening* has been embraced by critics who currently consider it a classic feminist text of American literature that argues against women's oppression and affirms women's liberation.

While Kelley has not been labeled a realist writer, her contributions to discussions about social prescriptions for women and representations of gender deserve exploration and recognition as invaluable intellectual contributions on marital discourse during the Age of Realism. Until quite recently, very little was known about Emma Kelley. One could argue that her portrait prefacing *Megda* appears to be racially inconclusive. "Such racial ambiguity reminds us that exteriority does not always reveal racial identity that visible signs cannot always serve as an epistemological guarantee."[13] Details of Kelley's life are sketchy, and most biographical information about her had been circumstantially pieced together. In 2005, Holly Jackson published an article in *The Boston Globe* entitled, "Mistaken Identity: What if a novelist celebrated as a pioneer of African-American women's literature turned out not to be black at all?" Puzzled by the lack of information to include in her entry to be published in the *African American National Biography*, Jackson, a graduate student of Brandeis University, did archival research on Kelley. Archival records uncovered by Jackson, which include birth and death records and census documents, suggest that Kelley was most likely white instead of black.

Due to this recent controversy surrounding Kelley's racial origin, she may become even further isolated from various literary traditions. The African-American literary tradition will inevitably have to release Kelley, while the American literary canon may not readily accept her with open arms. From a critical standpoint, how Kelley came to be identified as black is an urgent question that needs answering. Foiling Kelley against herself may lead to productive interrogation of her fluid racial identity and critical analysis of her novel's race politics. Reading Kelley as both a black and white author will challenge us to consider whether or not the literary value of her text depends upon her racial identity. Because the literary value and interest in Kelley's text hinges upon racial identity, critics overlook the importance of what *Megda* demonstrates regarding ideas and ideals of marriage. The novel clearly highlights what influence modern marriage had upon constructions of gender in the late nineteenth century. The insistent focus upon race causes the focus on the novel's gender politics to be lost. Kelley has not been read as a woman writer detached from racial politics. The case of Kelley reveals the danger of reading writers and their works through a lens of race. Kelley's *Megda* is an example of a rich text that is not overtly about racial concerns.

Read comparatively Kelley and Chopin's novels demonstrate how the dominant culture of late-nineteenth-century America regarded the institution of marriage. The marriage plot appealed to readers who could readily indulge in stories of courtship and fantasies of love. Yet writers often appropriated the marriage plot because it provided an acceptable forum for expressing their political positions to patriarchal and racially hierarchical orders in a non-threatening manner. *Megda* and *The Awakening* define marriage as a social institution, which solidifies a woman's civil status. However, both novels consider marriage as the foundation of the family. Marriage, then, is the mutual agreement between a man and woman to live together as husband and wife for civility. However, Kelley and Chopin complicate the assumption that marriage is the culminating event of a woman's life by revealing that marital love can be destructive if blinded by cultural prejudices and sexism. Protagonists Meg and Edna's fragmented identities are a result of the socially prescribed roles and community imposed values suffocating them. *Megda* and *The Awakening* demonstrate the individual growth and change in social position of Meg and Edna along their journeys of "awakening" and conversion. The tension between the secular and sacred resonates throughout both novels. In *Megda,* marriage is sacred, but in *The Awakening* secular meanings of marriage resonate throughout.

Emma Dunham-Kelley promotes the idea that a marriage results in happiness and fulfillment for a woman. Marriage becomes "a wonderful and powerful agent in the development and formation of a woman's character" in *Megda.*[14] Marriage becomes necessary for Meg to realize her worth and embrace a well-rounded identity. She can only fulfill the demands of her womanly nature within her marriage. Meg only comes to this realization after successfully resisting submission to God's spiritual calling upon her life. Because marriage is a sacred rite, Meg realizes that submission and not rebellion is required within the socioreligious institution of marriage. A woman does not become a truly fulfilled woman until she is married, just as a sinner cannot become a saint until there has been repentance and acceptance of salvation.

In its depiction of marriage as a sacred rite, *Megda* underscores the importance of the ceremonial rituals of baptism, courtship, graduation, and marriage. The novel continuously strives to reveal the tensions between the secular and the sacred. *Megda* clearly argues that traditional ideas of marriage have their basis in Christian theology. Marriage is a covenant with God before it is a covenant between man and wife. Marriage is first and foremost a religious rite of passage to salvation. Second, marriage is a rite of passage to womanhood. Marriage provides moral growth, healing, and protection for women. The fact that Kelley links marriage with religion supports her belief that marriage is not a social contract but a religious rite for passage. Meg simultaneously struggles to convert to Christianity and to marry. Allen Stein asserts "Marriage, particularly for a woman, involves a certain amount of submission."[15] Once she submits to the Christian faith, the pathway toward marriage is made clear. Kelley's Megda demonstrates that marriage can preserve the religious social order. Men and women can find comfort in marriage and still maintain appropriate patterns of social behavior. In the case of Meg and Reverend Stanley's marriage, there is a preservation of the social order, but a revision of the pattern of behavior. Meg is not a weak, submissive wife to a controlling husband. Meg and Rev. Stanley's partnership is based on camaraderie and friendship. "Marriage is the only equation where two halves do not make a whole. It requires two wholes."[16] Within their marriage, Meg and Rev. Stanley place emphasis on the preservation of each of their individual spirits and different identities in order for the marital union to work.

Megda focuses on the conversion of souls to Christ as opposed to men wooing women to love and marriage. Women can only become wholly and happy women by finding their spiritual identities. Marriage is equated with happiness and spiritual fulfillment for women in *Megda*. Emma Kelley overtly links marriage to Christianity's biblical imagery of Christ as the bridegroom and the church as Christ's bride.[17] This sacred metaphor of marriage between the bride and bridegroom reinforces traditional gender roles of men and women. A woman can only find happiness and fulfillment in marriage, for like Christ, her husband is her savior.[18] The husband is the head of the marital relationship and family, while the wife is submissive to his will.[19] Without a husband, a woman is lost. For she needs a husband to protect, guide, and "save" her.[20] Marriage sets up a hierarchical relationship where the husband is the head of the household even though he and his wife have joined as one.[21] Thus, a woman's identity becomes consumed within her husband's identity.

Megda affirms genteel ideals of womanhood. The plot and moral of the novel itself is propelled by the liberated and independent Meg's gradual transition into a life of subdued, Christian womanhood. The story of *Megda* chronicles its protagonist's struggle to convert to Christianity and secure a suitable marriage partner. Kelley clearly suggests that there is an appropriate process to transition from girlhood to womanhood. The narrator of the novel links a girl's coming of age with Christianity: "…but to me there is nothing as beautiful and altogether pleasing, as a sweet, fair, pure life at the time when 'girl-hood is about to pass through the window, and womanhood stands knocking at the door."[22] The novel articulates that the most appropriate way to make this transition from girlhood to womanhood is through the finding and connection with one's spiritual identity. "Happy they who 'remember their Creator in the days of their youth,' and early look to Him as their Guide and Protector through all the dark journey of life."[23] It is not until Meg finds her spiritual identity that she can embrace the secular rites of marriage and motherhood. Before she can embrace matrimony, Meg must sacrifice her worldly ways and individual autonomy.

Before her Christian conversion, Meg is a free, independent, and untamed secular woman. It is her Christian conversion that provides her with the genteel ideals of "true" womanhood. Throughout the novel Meg's mother, yearns for her daughter to convert and learn how to apply the tenets of true womanhood from her religion faith. Mrs. Randal lays out important secular and sacred concepts of true womanhood. She desires that her daughters grow up to be "good, pure, noble-minded women, respecting themselves and thus commanding respect from all with whom they come in contact."[24] Mrs. Randal wants her daughters to abide by this code of morals, for she considers morality and respect the two important ideals of womanhood. The idea that Christianity is an essential part of true womanhood is at the core of *Megda*'s argument. It is not until Meg finds her spiritual identity that she is able to embrace marriage and motherhood.

Meg is a likeable, demonstrative character for young women readers with aspirations of marriage. *Megda,* realist in intent, focuses on the complex temperament and motive of Meg and the complex ethical choices she must make in the midst of "coming of age" with her friends during senior year of high school. Out of the nine young women, Meg has the most difficult time settling into a pious and virtuous life. Meg must let go of her girlish ways before she can truly be a woman. Marriage, arguably, breaks bonds between women. The pursuit of marriage becomes a source of jealousy and competition between Meg and her high school friends.

Meg must acknowledge her dependence upon God, but her strong self-will makes her resistant to change. She takes pride in herself, and her vanity prevents her from relying on God. The attitude that Meg displays makes her unsuitable for marriage. She is not eligible for marriage because of her pride and immaturity. "Meg had always prided herself on her independent spirit; she had always found herself to be sufficient for her own comfort and happiness."[25] Because of her narcissism and proud nature, Meg does not have many friends, and even her so-called friends are sometimes her rivals. "She had never found it necessary, as the other girls had done, to depend on others—to look to others for help; she had always been proudly independent of everybody."[26] Meg considers her friends to be weak, and she treats them as if she does not need them.

Emma Kelley clearly suggests that Meg's persona is not the persona of an ideal wife. Meg is an example of a woman whose character needs to be tamed, and the novel seems to imply that marriage will somehow bring about this change in moral character. The following passage depicts Meg's difficulty submitting to religion, a source of patriarchal authority that will enable Meg can alter her character. "Religion will do for those who cannot depend on themselves; they are obliged to ask for help from somewhere—but what do I want of it? I am perfectly happy—have always been so—and what reason is there that I shall not always be so?"[27] Meg's prideful and selfish nature prevents her from recognizing that "she needed a Saviour's help."[28] As an autonomous and self-driven woman, Meg does not feel that she needs to be led by a man or saved by God. Yet Meg is only able to fulfill her romantic desires once she abandons her true feminine character to embrace religious authority.

The one true friend that Meg admires, Ethel, is the quintessential sentimental heroine. Ethel expresses individual strength and religious piety, and exhibits all the valuable traits of a wife to be. Ethel is eligible to marry in a way that Meg is not. Yet Meg admires Ethel because of her steadfast faith and commitment to God: "It seemed to her as if she were looking at one of God's angels."[29] Ethel represents the possibility of what Meg could be if she were to give up her worldly ways and turn her life over to God. The narrator, who praised Ethel's character, appears to exhibit bias as she condemns Meg's character: "Pride was Meg's besetting sin; it often kept her from converting noble thought into noble action."[30] Pride prevents Meg from true religious conversion, and it also delays her marital eligibility.

Meg is a good judge of everyone's characters except her own. For example, Meg finds Ruth passive and helpless, but fails to see her own pride and selfishness. Meg's brother Hal reminds her, "I have heard you say many times that...you admired character—you respected high ideas and lofty desires and noble pursuits; you despised weakness."[31] Hal admonishes Meg to remain consistent in her philosophy by judging a person's character based on the heart and not the exterior. "You had no respect for gentlemen, or ladies either, who never had a thought above dress and good times, and who couldn't do anything but giggle and talk silly nonsense."[32] Hal reminds Meg that what is on the inside is the most important indicator of character. Carla Peterson argues, "Kelley-Hawkins's valuation of character over personality; her condemnation of Meg's theatricality suggests that Meg is in danger of doing just the opposite, of valuing personality over character."[33] Meg often gets distracted by the performance aspects of an individual's personality and appearances. She loses sight of an individual's true moral and ethical character.

Ethel understands what Meg does not: the fading pleasures of the world can never compare to eternal happiness in Jesus. Meg finds that "religion is too severe…it makes mountains out of mole-hills."[34] She wants does not understand why she must give up "the social pleasures of the world" to become a devout Christian.[35] A central question posed by Emma Kelley's *Megda* seems to be, "How then can the Christian enjoy both outward from and inner spirit, while in the process of reconciling worldly Christian values?"[36] While Meg wants to remain connected to society, her acceptance of Christianity requires withdrawal from social pleasures of the world. Carla Peterson argues that Emma Kelley places emphasis on "the characters' enjoyment of worldliness just as they insist on an exploration of inner life through spiritual experiences of repentance and conversion."[37] This is evidenced by the fact that the narrator urges for the reader's pity of Meg's conflicted existence: "Poor Meg! She was as submissive a victim to the tyrant, pride."[38] Readers cannot help but feel sympathy for Meg's condition.

Meg stands by and watches her friends devote themselves to the Christian life. One-by-one, Meg's friends court, marry, and have children under the religious rules of proper behavior and decorum. Meanwhile, Meg remains distracted by the sensual and physical pleasures of the secular world. Because of her rebellion against many traditional gender roles, Meg is the last one of the group to finally be saved. She tells Ethel she will enter the school of matrimony after high school: "I tell you, Ethel, when I get through this school of education, I am going to enter the one of matrimony, just about as quickly as I can, and you may be very sure that the all-important man will be a rich one."[39] Meg finds an education on how to marry well more valuable than any book learning. For Meg, marriage is the key to social advancement and material gain, but Ethel quickly reminds her that she already possesses the keys to happiness outside of marriage. "'I do not like to hear you talk in this way, Girlie. You are capable of great things'"[40] Ethel tries to deter Meg from thinking that marriage will bring happiness, wholeness, and money.

Emma Kelley appears to critique social culture which promotes women as ornaments for men and doormats for marriage. Women must be determined to define themselves in a society that seeks to define and control them. Kelley prioritizes women's pursuit of their own educational and professional security before marriage by underscoring the dangers of women relying upon marriage as a security blanket. By novel's end, Meg becomes Ethel metaphorically. She transforms from a worldly woman into a woman defined by the patriarchal standards of society and religion. Meg sets her sights on a sacred marriage, and she sheds her desire for a marriage defined by social position and money. Meg promises Ethel on her deathbed that she will marry Reverend Stanley.

Emma Kelley places select emphasis on Meg's marriage to a clergyman as a manifestation of her successful conversion. At the request of her friend Maude, who also dies an untimely death, Meg adopts her daughter. Meg also has two children of her own with Rev. Stanley, and the success of their marriage is demonstrated through the fact that they have been fruitful and multiplied.[41] Rev. Stanley suggests that Meg has grown spiritually in her commitment to God through her selfless dedication to both family and community. "Her life was filled up with work—noble work—in her love and in the world outside."[42] However, even though Meg winds up in the socially sanctioned roles of wife and mother, she is not the object of Rev. Stanley's possession. Their love is not a love of flesh but a love of the spirit. Meg finds the solidification of her faith in matrimony. Her marital relationship with Rev. Stanley is egalitarian. The Stanley marriage subverts the gender expectations of the husband dominating a submissive wife. Meg maintains her "independent spirit" despite the fact that she has "a tender, loving husband to guide and protect her."[43] Though initially, marriage has absolutely nothing to do with religious sanctity, by novel's end Meg is finally able to reconcile sacred and secular ideologies of marriage. The novel has a high regard for moral and ethical character.

Even though there are features of realism evident in the character development of Meg, the happy marriage Emma Kelley depicts at the end of *Megda* is strictly romantic in convention. Whereas the failed marriage that Kate Chopin depicts in *The Awakening* is strictly realist in convention. It rejects the definition of marriage as happiness and fulfillment for women. Chopin attacks marriage, "which by its very nature does not place individual fulfillment above ties to others."[44] Marriage is simply another form of oppression perpetuated upon women that results in a further divide between the sexes. Chopin highlights the gender inequality and resulting consequences of the alleged "storybook" marriage, where the supposedly perfectly matched husband and wife live harmoniously and happily-ever-after.[45] In *The Awakening*, we see the failed possibility of love developing later on in a lifeless marriage of convenience whose basis is in the social contract of consumer American culture.[46] The unromantic marriage of Edna and Mr. Pontellier that is based on pragmatic accommodation starts out as a marriage of convenience. Marriage is a desired marker of social identification for the Pontelliers before Edna begins to comprehend the flaws of her idealized vision of marriage. Chopin overtly links marriage to a society based on social contract. The Pontellier marriage is observed by a society, which seeks to determine whether the parties involved are observing the manners and customs required of them as husband, wife, and productive citizens of society. This is an example of the private sphere of marriage in a very public domain. Chopin succeeds at "devaluating marriage as character-shaping and society-sustaining institution."[47] Chopin presents the inevitability of marriage stifling the feminine identity of her protagonist Edna. Edna is not a submissive woman, so she rebels against the demands married life places upon her. *The Awakening* focuses on the suffering and pain within a marriage in a society that commodifies and prevents women from liberating themselves. It is clear that Chopin considers marriage "valid only insofar as it allows the individuals to attain self-fulfillment."[48] Edna is neither able to maintain a fulfilling life nor find an authentic identity as a married woman.

Kate Chopin defines marriage as a social contract in a society motivated by a capitalist system of exchange and production. Marriage, moreover, is a requirement of consumer culture in Edna's desire for wealth, class, and social status. An ill-advised marriage between Edna and her husband Mr. Pontellier, who are compatible in terms of class status, never becomes completely harmonious. Chopin seems to suggest that choices in marriage have serious consequences, not only for the individual parties at stake but also for society at large. In its demonstration that the choice of a marriage partner is serious business, *The Awakening* looks at the effects of matrimony on society. The novel reveals that short romantic courtships that result in marriages based upon class status and social mobility lead to divorce. Both parties entertain unrealistic ideals of one another and marry without getting to know one another. The unfortunate result is a clash between the male and female will. What remains is a dissolved marriage and two wrecked lives. Though Kate Chopin upholds the value of marriage as an institution, she is pessimistic about successful marital relationships between men and women.

There are three points of focus in Kate Chopin's characterization of marriage in *The Awakening*: the benefits of marriage, problems that can occur in marriage, and marital entrapment. The unromantic Pontellier marriage appears to be based upon convenience and accommodation. Mr. Pontellier looks at his wife Edna "as one looks at a valuable piece of personal property."[49] Mr. Pontellier loves Edna but treats her as if she is a decorative ornament. Kate Chopin explores the consequences women face when they buy into the myth of the "storybook" marriage and allow themselves to become exploited commodities on the "marriage market."[50] She rejects the idea that marriage is a necessary step to achieving womanhood. For Edna there is no such thing as marital bliss. "There were days when she was unhappy, she did not know why."[51] Marriage is filled with unhappiness and unfulfillment for Edna, who "could not have told why she was crying. Such experiences as the foregoing were not uncommon in her married life."[52] Though she is married, Edna is alone as she struggles to cope with the demands placed upon her by marriage. Chopin appears to argue that marriage is an oppressive institution that furthers the divide between the sexes. Clearly, marriage is not a relationship that can promote legitimate self-expression and personal development in the case of Edna. Chopin asserts that marriage breaks woman-centered development. Marriage is the point where individual male and female identities inevitably collide with zero chance of reconciliation or repair.

The Awakening tells the story of Edna, a privileged aristocrat from New Orleans. While on vacation at Grande Isle with her husband and children, Edna meets and falls in love with young Robert Lebrun. Lebrun teaches Edna how to swim. Adele Ratignolle, a woman Edna befriends, realizes that Edna may misunderstand the relationship. She warns Robert that Edna, "is not one of us; she is not like us. She might make the unfortunate blunder of taking you seriously."[53] Edna is not Creole; therefore, she does not know how to interpret Creole cultural gestures. Adele warns Robert that Edna may take his flirtation seriously.

Though she never truly fits into the Creole society, Edna does what is expected of her as a woman, and she admires the Creole people's "absence of prudery" and "freedom of expression."[54] Edna begins painting and enjoys indulging in music to freely express her repressed emotions, new-found strength, and individual creativity. "In short, Mrs. Pontellier was beginning to realize her position in the universe as a human being, and to recognize her relations as an individual to the world within and about her."[55] Edna awakens with new life, but she is unable to fit back into either of her social roles as wife and mother once she returns to New Orleans. When Edna tries to verbalize her need for independence and self-expression, she meets resistance.

Edna befriends two women who typify Creole culture, Mademoiselle Reisz, and Madame Ratignolle. These two women represent two different models for the Creole life Edna could possibly settle into. A single woman on the outskirts of society's prescription for women, Mademoiselle Reisz listens to Edna without judging her. She knows Edna's true feelings for Robert, and she encourages Edna to connect with herself individually by tapping into her creative skills. A loner leading a Bohemian lifestyle, Mademoiselle Reisz is detached from the community because she has dedicated her life to her heart's passion, music. She has chosen a life of art and culture over the more traditional roles of marriage and motherhood. Edna admires Mademoiselle Reisz's courage, for she has made the distinct choice not to marry or have children. Mademoiselle Reisz warns Edna that a true artist must be a brave soul and be willing to function on the margins of society. Mademoiselle Reisz may be the more influential of the two women in Edna's process of awakening because she is not married and does not have children. Edna desperately wants to revert to this type of single lifestyle.

By contrast, Madame Ratignolle is a typical Creole woman who is devoted to her family and dependent upon her husband. She exemplifies the lifestyle that Edna so desperately wants to escape. A woman of elegance and charm, Adele Ratignolle teaches Edna how to embrace freedom and self-expression. Adele is forthright and unreserved by example. She encourages Edna to express her emotions and desires. Adele represents the Victorian ideal of the happily married woman with children. She centers her life upon her husband, children, and domestic duties. Adele "was the embodiment of every womanly grace and charm…there are no words to describe her save the old ones that have served so often to picture the bygone heroine of romance and the fair lady of our dreams."[56] Edna is attracted to Adele because of her "excessive physical charm" and the "candor of the woman's whole existence."[57] Adele is a "mother-woman."[58] She is not sexually awakened like Edna, but her Creole conversation is full of free discourse about love, sex, and childbirth. Adele's openness inspires Edna to abandon her initial reserved and introverted personality. She gives Edna, for whom "a certain light was beginning to dawn dimly within" the vocabulary to openly voice her desires.[59]

The narrator reveals that Edna's marriage to Mr. Pontellier was "purely an accident…resembling many other marriages which masquerade as the decrees of Fate."[60] Chopin underscores the abundance of marriages in name and deed only, for marriage more often than not meant partnership, contract, and social advancement. However, Edna's marriage to Mr. Pontellier appears to be the perfect, fated marriage even though it is actually an accidental occurrence. Their performed courtship suggests that the practice of marriage is an art. The Pontellier's eventual marriage is described an illusion at best: "He fell in love, as men are in the habit of doing, and pressed his suit with an earnestness and an ardor which left nothing to be deserved. He pleased her; his absolute devotion flattered her."[61] Mr. Pontellier falls in love, not Edna. The narrator's commentary indicates that men instead of women fall in love easily. Edna marries her husband only because "she fancied there was a sympathy of thought and taste between them."[62] Edna does not marry her husband because they share the passion of a fairytale romance. By choosing to marry for the practical reasons of social and financial stability, Edna shuts the door on love and romance. As a result, her relationship with Mr. Pontellier is based on a system of barter and exchange. Chopin clearly comments upon the social behaviors between men and women that can lead to illusive marriages.

Edna is oppressed by a society that demands her conformity to the behavioral norms of wife and mother. Scientific discourse in the novel suggests that inherited biological character traits may be the reason for Edna's flaws. The narrator insinuates that Edna is tainted by bad stock. Notably, Edna has problems with every man in her life, including her father, husband, lover (Alcee Arobin), and near lover (Robert Lebrun). At various moments in the novel, Edna is owned by all these men who seek to control and define her "by those assumptions about women she seeks vainly to escape."[63] Mr. Pontellier regards Edna as his possession or a valuable piece of property. She becomes a symbol of his social status. Mr. Pontellier represents the conformity of society, while Edna retreats from society. Mr. Pontellier, desperate to keep up with social appearances, places an ad in the paper indicating that their house is being remodeled. This is his way of hiding Edna's actions from the community. Edna views her departure from the Pontellier house as a self-ordained divorce from her marriage vows. The narrator remarks that Edna feels lower on the social totem pole. "There was with her a feeling of having descended in the social scale, with a corresponding sense of having risen in the spiritual."[64] While Edna has descended on a social scale, she has transcended spiritually. Because Edna's place in society is defined by marriage, her retreat from the socially binding marriage contract not only facilitates her fall from social standing but also strengthens her spiritual connection with herself.

In *The Awakening*, marriage is the equivalent of entrapment, and the novel traces Edna's escapes from the confines of her caged existence. Though Mr. Pontellier takes for granted that Edna will remain faithful to her marriage vows and respect the social mores of Creole culture, Edna chooses to ignore her marriage vows. Mr. Pontellier cannot imagine Edna having an affair, and upon consultation with Dr. Mandelet, his worries about Edna are put to rest. The doctor advises Mr. Pontellier, "Woman, my dear friend, is a very peculiar and delicate organism… most women are moody and whimsical."[65] The doctor's diagnosis of Edna mirrors the popular notion that women are defined by their emotions, which can then lead to hysteria and madness.

Dr. Mandelet assures Mr. Pontellier there is nothing wrong with Edna, for he concludes that Edna is simply going through a passing phase, and "it will pass happily over, especially if you left her alone."[66] Dr. Madelet's prescription for Edna's "condition" echoes the "rest cure" prescribed for Charlotte Perkins Gilman's emotionally and mentally unwell protagonist in "The Yellow Wall-Paper" (1891). There is no possibility that Edna is literally going through an identity crisis because it is assumed that wifehood and motherhood are the culminating makers of her complete happiness and feminine identity. Though he treats Edna well, Mr. Pontellier does not know her true feelings and emotions. His only concern is with appearances and the community's impressions of Edna's behavior.

In a society that demands adherence to social codes and gender roles, death is the only option for Edna's escape. Edna has an affair with Alcee Arobin, a man known for pursuing adulterous relationships with married women. Edna divorces herself from an unhappy marriage with Mr. Pontellier and moves on without legally dissolving her marriage. Arobin arouses Edna's desire for sexual passion, a thing absent from her marriage with Mr. Pontellier. Arobin's brief attempt to satisfy Edna's sexual needs is unsuccessful because Edna truly loves Robert. Because Robert has a morally grounded respect for the sacredness of marriage, he rejects Edna's proposition of love.

Even if awakening to the truth mandates future suffering, Edna is content knowing that she is no longer living in a dream world: "The years that are gone seem like dreams—if one might go on sleeping and dreaming—but to wake up and find—oh! well! Perhaps it is better to wake up after all, even to suffer, rather than to remain a dupe to illusions all one's life."[67] Because the society Edna exists within allows for little compromise between the two extremes of individuality and social prescription, Edna is tossed to and fro like the waves of the sea that engulf her in death. Edna no longer maintains a place in the social world or the literal world for that matter. Sadly, there is no happily-ever-after for Edna, for she commits suicide. For Edna, "The voice of the sea is seductive, never ceasing, whispering, clamoring, murmuring, inviting the soul to wander in abysses of solitude."[68] Edna gives herself to the sea, which symbolizes her freedom. Edna's submergence into the sea symbolizes baptism, and her awakening is described in overt religious overtones of rebirth.

Edna's baptismal cleansing ritual transforms her into a re-born woman. Edna experiences a baptism by suicide when she drowns herself in the ocean. Death is the only means by which Edna can obtain freedom, for she has exhausted the possibilities of the literal world. "If *The Awakening* begins with a domestic space carved out from the masculine world, it ends with an oceanic maternal space that negates the entire world."[69] The ocean water of Edna's suicidal demise bears similarity to the amniotic fluid of a mother's womb. Like a mother, the sea rocks Edna in the cradle of its arms. This image serves as a reminder that Edna has not escaped the maternal role that she so desperately wants to leave behind.

There are a number of striking parallels and differences between Meg and Edna. Meg and Edna yearn for the position in life that the other already possesses. Meg is a young adult woman quite like Edna, if we care to imagine what Edna was like before her marriage to Mr. Pontellier. Spunky, independent, and self-driven, Meg rebels against society's prescription for what women can and cannot do. Meg enjoys playing cards, dancing, music, and theater. These are activities that her church condemns. She is a virtuous woman, but does not want to let go of the social pleasures that she likes to engage in. Initially, Meg struggles with the fact that her acceptance into the religious social order is contingent upon the sacrifice of her individuality. She faces a conflict between her love for social pastimes and Christianity. However, Meg finds solace in her spiritual conversion and marriage to Rev. Stanley. She is satisfied with taking her proper place as Christian, wife, and mother.

Edna, by contrast, is a middle-aged woman who transgresses the boundaries of the domestic. Like Meg initially, Edna is a worldly woman who is spunky, independent, and unique. Edna, like Meg, rebels against the society's bourgeois values for women. Arguably, she has two extra-marital affairs. While there are no literal religious concerns at stake in *The Awakening*, religious metaphors define Edna's journey of awakening most clearly. Chopin uses religious metaphorical language to intensify the sacredness of Edna's journey toward social transcendence and feminine autonomy. Unlike Meg, Edna is not on a journey toward religious consciousness or salvation. She journeys toward the awakening of her individual self, which contains a spirituality of its own. Edna tries to discover the woman she truly is. During her season of marriage and motherhood, Edna is oblivious to her individual self. Yet Edna's awakening can be characterized by her newly found desire to be a woman outside of society's delineation of women's roles as wives and mothers. She yearns for Meg's initial social status as an unmarried woman. If we appropriate the religious metaphor of life as a journey, Edna fails to convert to marriage and motherhood because she does not complete the journey. Her conversion is a short-lived one, for she walks away from her family, society, and eventually retreats from the world altogether. Edna divorces herself from marriage, motherhood, and finally from life itself.

Meg, by contrast, yearns to be in a social position that we understand to be Edna's. Meg wants to be married, for she believes in the fairytale romance. Furthermore, she knows that marriage will make her an honest woman and secure her social position in society. Yet Meg, like Edna, wants neither to give up her autonomy nor to compromise her identity. Meg buys into the social order of a community that stipulates she can only truly discover herself as a woman through religious awakening. She yearns to graduate from the single lifestyle that Edna so desperately wants to retreat from her marriage back into. The new-found spiritual wisdom of Meg's youth enables her to give up her worldly ways to embrace faith and the sacred rights of womanhood. She happily relinquishes her pride and individual autonomous will to convert to religious faith, marriage, and motherhood.

Edna, by contrast, is never able to find that balance. She moves from the sacred space of the home to the secular space of society. Once Edna leaves her husband and children, she is no longer protected by the safety and security that marriage and motherhood bring. Edna moves into her own house where she isolates herself and sinks into further depression and solitude. Edna faces a conflict between her love for the arts and individual autonomy versus her job as a wife and mother. Edna discovers that if she wants to attend to her individual self, society mandates that she must give up her marriage and family; however, if Edna wants to be a good mother, then she must give up her passion for art and individuality. Edna's tragedy is that she cannot find a happy medium between the two societal extremes. Edna's independence as a woman and roles of wife and mother are diametrically opposed in a society that does not honor women's individuality.

Meg and Edna's baptisms transform them. Meg's literal baptism symbolizes her transformation from sinner to saint. She is dead to her secular ways and born into a new Christian way of life. Meg joins with the church and God eternally. Her baptism foreshadows her eventual union with Reverend Arthur Stanley. Meg is cleansed from her old life as a single, lost young woman and reborn into a life of wisdom and piety. Edna, on the contrary, experiences a baptism by suicide. Death is the only means by which Edna can obtain freedom, for she has exhausted the possibilities of the literal world.

Both *Megda* and *The Awakening* are novels about death more so than they are about life. While Meg and Edna experience social conversions and individual awakenings, they also pay the high cost of death. Notably, both protagonists make the conscious choice to die from a former prescribed identity to embrace a new autonomous one. Meg symbolically dies from her worldly nature and becomes a spiritually converted woman. Edna must experience a literal death in order to be free of society's prescriptions. Arguably, Edna is a dying woman before she commits suicide. The society she is trapped within stifles her feminine identity and creativity. Edna is suffocated by the social mores and pressures to conform to a society that fails to recognize her autonomy.

Meg and Edna make decisive breaks with social codes prescribed for women in patriarchal societies that promote chauvinism and demand women's conformity. *Megda* and *The Awakening* offer criticisms of women's subordination and biological determinism. Kelley and Chopin employ fictions of gender to expose marriage for what it is worth, an institution isolating men and women into separate categories of difference. The two novels demonstrate that marriage is often clouded by fictions of gender that delegate masculine and feminine roles of identity. As a result, the two novels also expose the dangers of marriage functioning as a dividing line instead of facilitating union between the sexes.

Culture of late nineteenth-century America regarded the institution of marriage as sacred and as secular. The marriage plot appealed to readers who could readily indulge in stories of courtship and fantasies of love. Yet writers often appropriated the marriage plot because it provided an acceptable forum for expressing their political positions in a nonthreatening manner to patriarchal and racially hierarchical orders. Definitions of marriage in *Megda* and *The Awakening* are centered upon class. Class is important to the realist novel that serves the interests and aspirations of an insurgent middle class. Meg and Edna are portrayed in contrast to the respective societies they each exist within.

Emma Dunham Kelly's *Megda* and Kate Chopin's *The Awakening* depict marriage as a viable part of the social order, but acknowledge that even well-intentioned marital love can be destructive if blinded by the cultural prejudice of sexism. Both novels express concern regarding the influence of patriarchy on women's lives by using realism to explore their heroines' relationships to social worlds and the conflicts therein. Kelley argues that women can find comfort and even maintain their own individual identities within marriage in spite of society's promotion of sexist values and traditional gender roles. While Chopin argues that for better or worse, women's individual needs will assert themselves in a marriage. Both Kelley and Chopin agree that women's identities as wives and mothers are imposed gender roles.

Marriage is a social institution, which solidifies a woman's civil status and the foundation of the family in both *Megda* and *The Awakening*. However, both novels define marriage as the mutual agreement between a man and woman to live together as husband and wife for civility. Kelley and Chopin complicate the assumption that marriage is the culminating event of a woman's life. Marital love can be destructive if it is blinded by individual desires. Love of God becomes the primary sources of marital satisfaction in *Megda*. In *The Awakening*, we see that it is a lack of love that easily destroys a marriage based on social contract. Protagonists Meg Randal and Edna Pontellier's fragmented identities are a result of the socially prescribed roles and community imposed values suffocating them. Meg and Edna's senses of identity are based upon their positions in a society that demands women's conformity.

Notes

1. Ann duCille, *The Coupling Convention: Sex, Text, and Tradition in Black Women's Fiction* (New York: Oxford University Press, 1993), 65.
2. Nancy F. Cott, *Public Vows: A History of Marriage and the Nation* (Cambridge: Harvard University Press, 2000), 63.
3. Stephanie Coontz, *Marriage, a History: How Love Conquered Marriage* (New York: Penguin, 2005), 35.
4. Milton C. Regan, Jr., *Alone Together: Law and the Meanings of Marriage* (New York: Oxford University Press, 1999), 7.
5. Coontz, 86.
6. Dating the time period of realism has been a source of debate among scholars of American literary realism. Many critics and scholars will label the realist period as early as 1860 and sometimes as late as the year 1920. Those critics that suggest the period begins in 1860 often argue that the period ends as early as 1890. Some critics argue that realism begins right at the time of the Civil War, 1865, but find the features and influences of realism extending well beyond the nineteenth-century into twentieth-century modernist texts.
7. Teresa C. Zackodnik, *The Mulatta and the Politics of Race* (Jackson: University of Mississippi Press, 2004), 77.
8. Elsa Nettels, *Language, Race, and Social Class in Howells's America* (Lexington: University Press of Kentucky, 1988), 5.
9. "Masking" is a trope in African-American literature defined as the rhetorical strategy of signifying or subverting to make empowering political commentary on race

concerns in a racially prejudged context. Paul Laurence Dunbar's famous poem, "We Wear the Mask," describes how late nineteenth-century African-Americans perform being black. Dunbar's rich imagery metaphorically captures how blacks hide the painfully oppressive reality of being black in an injustice America behind smiling masks that disclose feelings of anger, grief, and sadness.

10. See chapter four of Barbara Hochman, *Getting at the Author: Reimagining Books and Reading in the Age of Realism* (Amherst: University of Massachusetts Press, 2001) for a full discussion of the realist woman writer's self-consciousness about writing professionally and worries about the public reception of her work.
11. Augusta Rohrbach, *Truth Stranger Than Fiction: Race, Realism, and the U.S. Literary Marketplace* (New York: Palgrave, 2002), 104.
12. Barbara Welter, *Dimity Convictions: The American Woman in the Nineteenth-Century* (Columbus: University of Ohio Press, 1976) discusses the cult of true womanhood as a nineteenth-century ideology of womanhood that promoted piety, domesticity, virtue, and purity. This was primarily an ideology of white womanhood. Many black women aspired toward this ideology, but the institution of slavery and its practices often prevented these tenets from coming to fruition for them.
13. Carla Peterson, "New Negro Modernity: Worldliness and Interiority in the Novels of Emma Dunham Kelley-Hawkins," *Women's Experience of Modernity, 1875–1945,* Ed. Ann L. Ardis (Baltimore: Johns Hopkins University Press, 2003), 113.
14. Allen F. Stein, *After the Vows Were Spoken: Marriage in American Literary Realism* (Columbus: Ohio State University Press, 1984), 181.
15. *Ibid.,* 176.
16. Johnny Parker, *Blueprints for Marriage: Building Love for a Lifetime* (Lanham, MD: PnumaLife Publishers, 2002), 5–6.
17. See Revelations 21:2 in the *New International Version Study Bible.* Christ is often referred to as the bridegroom and the church is commonly referred to Christ's bride. John describes The New Jerusalem after the Millennium period where Christ receives his church unto himself as a husband receives his bride.
18. See Ephesians 5:22–23 in *The New International Version Student Bible* for a discussion of the spiritual relationship between wives and husbands.
19. See 1 Peter 3:1–2.
20. See Ephesians 5: 25–28.
21. See Genesis 2:24.
22. Emma Dunham Kelley-Hawkins, Megda, Ed. Henry Louis Gates, Jr. (New York: Oxford University Press, 1988). 227.
23. *Ibid.*
24. *Ibid.,* 55.
25. *Ibid.,* 102.
26. *Ibid.*
27. *Ibid.*

28. *Ibid.*
29. *Ibid.*, 224.
30. *Ibid.*, 102.
31. *Ibid.*, 59.
32. *Ibid.*
33. Peterson, 122.
34. Kelley-Hawkins, 167.
35. *Ibid.*
36. Peterson, 125.
37. Kelley-Hawkins, 113.
38. *Ibid.*, 104.
39. *Ibid.*, 12.
40. *Ibid.*
41. See Genesis 1:22.
42. Kelley-Hawkins, 394.
43. Kelley-Hawkins, 102, 394.
44. Stein, 165.
45. By "storybook," I mean the conventional fairytale ending that we find at the end of romantic novels or "boy-meets-girl" tales, where two perfectly matched individuals are fated to meet, marry, have children and live happily-ever-after.
46. See Amy Kaplan, *The Social Construction of American Realism* (Chicago: University of Chicago Press, 1988) for further discussion about realism as a strategy for "imagining and managing the threats of social change" (411). Kaplan writes about realist writers' works emphasis on consumer American culture, for as writers they considered themselves to be part of the social and political upheavals taking place in society. Kaplan argues that realist writers felt that their works were interventions that mediated and influenced shifts in various belief and value systems including marriage.
47. Stein, 166.
48. *Ibid.*, 176.
49. Kate Chopin, *The Awakening*, Ed. Margo Culley (New York: W. W. Norton, 1994), 4.
50. Augusta Rohrbach, *Truth Stranger Than Fiction: Race, Realism, and the U.S. Literary Marketplace* (New York: Palgrave, 2002), 104.
51. Chopin, 56.
52. *Ibid.*, 8.
53. *Ibid.*, 20.
54. *Ibid.*, 10.
55. *Ibid.*, 14.
56. *Ibid.*, 9.
57. *Ibid.*, 14.
58. *Ibid.*, 9.

59. *Ibid.*, 14.
60. *Ibid.*, 18.
61. *Ibid.*
62. *Ibid.*
63. Anna Shannon Elfenbein, *Women on the Color Line: Evolving Stereotypes and the Writings of George Washington Cable, Grace King, Kate Chopin* (Charlottesville: University Press of Virginia, 1989), 143.
64. Chopin, 89.
65. *Ibid.*, 63–64.
66. *Ibid.*, 64.
67. *Ibid.*, 105.
68. *Ibid.*, 108.
69. Elizabeth Fox-Genovese, "Progression and Regression in Edna Pontellier," *The Awakening*, Ed. Margo Culley (New York: W. W. Norton, 1994), 258.

Chapter 2

Marriage on the "Color Line" in Frances E. W. Harper's *Iola Leroy* and William Dean Howells's *An Imperative Duty*

Realist literature of the late-nineteenth-century United States provided a forum for discussions of "race." Because race could not be visually measured, the category of race was obviously unstable. The binary distinction of race, white and non-white, was not always clear. One means by which racial difference was both validated and quantified was the idea of inherited racial character.[1] "Character" referred to an individual's moral fiber or the belief system by which he or she operated. During the Age of Realism, character and race were often used as synonymous references to an individual's traits, behavior, and origin.[2]

How traits of a race were inherited became the focal point of scientific and philosophical inquiry in the nineteenth century. "Mid-nineteenth-century white American minds were fertile ground for the contention that biology dictated character and behavior. This biologizing of character was a cornerstone of the ideology of fundamental racial difference, and the rhetoric white Americans found most appealing was a sentimental, or romantic, racialism."[3] Literary realism promoted and questioned a scientific discourse of heredity that sought to categorize racial attributes and classify identity and character. In literature, mulattos often symbolized racial ambiguity and blurred the boundary of the "color line," for they pointed to the fact that the visual was an inefficient way to determine race or character. Teresa Zackodnik argues, "A variety of nineteenth-and twentieth-century scientific studies and popular understandings of the effects of 'blood admixture' attributed ostensibly greater intelligence in mulattas to their white blood, while less significant 'traits' or 'detriments' were traced to their black blood."[4]

Because *An Imperative Duty* was published a year before Harper's *Iola Leroy*, many critics have indicated that Harper's *Iola Leroy* is a direct response and even rewriting of Howells's *An Imperative Duty*. Instead of describing the relationship between these two novels in such a manner, I find it more useful to think of these two texts as call-and-response.[5] Frances Harper published *Minnie's Sacrifice*, a shorter version of *Iola Leroy*, in 1869. Published as a serialized novel in *The Christian Recorder* twenty-two years before Howells's *An Imperative Duty*, *Minnie's Sacrifice* deals with the issues of racial identity and racial duty. Minnie and Louis, the two mulatto protagonists of the novel, discover their true racial identities on the eve of the Civil War. Minnie and Louis decide to embrace their black heritage and dedicate their lives to the cause of racial uplift. Unlike Iola, Minnie loses her life for the racial uplift cause that she has embraced. Minnie and Iola become two kinds of heroines. Minnie dies a martyr for the race cause, while Iola lives happily-ever-after leading a life in service to the race. As meta-critical works, William Dean Howells's *An Imperative Duty* (1891) and Frances E. W. Harper's *Iola Leroy* (1892) demonstrate the difficulty authors faced when trying to fictionally represent race and the "color line."

A term loosely thrown around in mid-to-late-nineteenth-century America, the "color line," had two distinct meanings. First, it referred to the line of distinction drawn between people socially identified as members of the black race and white race. Second, the "color line" represented a boundary that should not be crossed for fear that the whole race would become impure due to the intermingling of white and black blood. In *A Question of Character*, Cathy Boeckmann states, "According to scientific understandings of racial difference, when white blood mingled with that of other races the resulting offspring were inferior to the white parent."[6] "Unsurprisingly, then, atavism was a popular fear associated with miscegenation."[7] "If this happened on a larger scale, the race as a whole would be degraded."[8] For fear of white racial impurity, the strict separation of the races was a situation for why the "color line" was invented. "'Blood' proves to be the omnipotent image associated with theories of race throughout the history of the construction of race in America."[9]

The "color line" maintained its basis on the principle of hypodescent. The principle of hypodescent stipulates that even an individual who is only a small fraction black is considered entirely black despite the larger fraction of whiteness possessed.[10] David Hollinger argues that "blackness in the Unites States is an ascribed status, imposed on a spectrum of color shades and descent percentages, rather than a category of nature."[11] Despite the principle of hypodescent's monolithic notion of blackness, mulattos were often always described as being on the "color line," a space of existence between the black and white races. Since there was no socially recognized middle ground, mulattos had to cast their lot with either the white or the black race. "Since the color line was justified on the basis of a supposed instinctual desire to preserve the blood purity of the white race, the people on the color line stood as ironic statements to the inconsistent influence of that instinct."[12]

George W. Stocking describes the "nineteenth-century sense of 'race' as accumulated cultural differences carried somehow in the blood."[13] David Hollinger argues, "The stigma carried by blackness is unique, and is affixed and perpetuated resolutely."[14] Ultimately, both Harper and Howells's novels complicate the ever-popular "one-drop" rule through explorations of the identity crises mixed-raced protagonists Iola Leroy and Rhoda Aldgate embody. Both writers offer commentary on the science behind an assumption that one could measure the amount of black blood in a mixed-race individual and determine his or her racial category. Harper and Howells's differing positions on the "one-drop" rule is a direct reflection of the political shifts taking place in race relations during the post-Reconstruction era. Harper and Howells, to a lesser degree, try to move beyond the stock romantic figure of the tragic mulatto popular among their white contemporaries' texts.

Where Harper succeeds in critiquing and rejecting the racial stereotype of the tragic mulatto, Howells's attempt simply reinforces the stereotyped characterization. In Howells's depiction of Rhoda's character, her black blood can only be a negative instead of a positive influence on her whiteness. For Harper, the "one-drop" rule was more a matter of social value. Iola must decide not which "blood" she will be true to, but whether she will either be true to the material value of financial prosperity embodied in whiteness, or to the moral value of ethical duty embodied in blackness.

Marriage is also a central subject of nineteenth-century fiction. The literal marriages that take place in both novels function as metaphors for the proposed union between opposites in social, political, and cultural realms. The "color line" was a representation for the boundaries between polar opposites that was to discourage marriages between black and white. Marriage was not only a religious rite; it was also a legal contract that often determined an individual's identity, autonomy, and in some cases, ownership of property. Failure to recognize the marriages of African Americans meant covert denial of their legal rights.

Both Harper and Howells use mulatto figures to embody fictional representations of "race" as they criticize popular racial scientific ideology behind the "one-drop" rule. Both authors choose marriage, the highest moral act of commitment between a man and woman, as the backdrop for their different commentaries on the "one-drop" rule. Both Harper and Howells use their characters' moral decisions and ethical choices surrounding marriage as realist narrative strategy to express the possibility for racial utopia, while simultaneously exposing the impossibility of that vision. Upon finding out her true racial identity, Rhoda chooses to pass as white for the remainder of her life, while Iola quickly aligns herself with her black heritage. Iola and Rhoda's decisions about which racial heritage they will align with directly influence their choices of marriage partners. For Harper, the egalitarianism of a marital union between a black man and a black woman symbolizes an optimistic possibility for racial harmony in an ideal society. Conversely, the interracial marriage between Rhoda and Olney in *An Imperative Duty* represents a major obstacle to a racially harmonious society.

Harper places her story in significant historical context. On the eve of the Civil War, Iola discovers that she is of mixed-race heritage. The narrator describes the national state of affairs at the beginning of chapter three: "The Union had snapped asunder because it lacked the cohesion of justice, and the Nation was destined to pass through the crucible of disaster and defeat, till she was ready to clasp hands with the Negro and march abreast with him to freedom and victory."[15] This passage clearly suggests that Iola's story is a story of America. The "race problem" takes on national proportions, for it is not merely a "black" problem but an American problem. Harper blends fact and fiction to rewrite history from a distinctly black woman's perspective.

Iola is a historical figure representing a reality of slavery, segregation, racism, and liberation experienced by some black women. Through Iola's experiences, Harper's multiple audiences of readers come to understand challenges some black women faced during and immediately after the Civil War. "By titling her novel after her heroine rather than after a duty larger than the individual, Harper announces the importance of a single character, and a woman no less."[16] Claudia Tate argues, "The novel uses the mulatto's inherent transitional racial and class status to construct emancipatory resocialization, grounded in virtue, education, and hard work."[17] Iola chooses to accept her racial designation, and the iconic status of Iola affirms the historical importance of the novel. Iola is a fictional creation representative of not just one particular black woman, but many mulatto women on the "color line."

The mulatto character was a manifestation of sexual relations between the races. As a historical marker of institutionalized racism and the separation of the races, the mulatto character was a useful vehicle for exploring race relations and class issues. The mulatto's racial fluidity afforded her or him the opportunity for social mobility into the upper class. Because American culture valorized whiteness, the female mulatto character appealed especially to white women readers because she embodied ideals of white beauty. White women's identification with mulatto women characters made discussions of racism and sexism easier. Harper presents an emotionally stirring account of history that aims to bring about racial awareness and encourage "race" reform. Although remanded to slavery, Iola survives sexual harassment and indignities by white men. She restores herself to her family and community. Harper purposely fails to place *Iola Leroy*'s primary focus on slavery, yet she deliberately produces a counter narrative of slavery. She appeals to sympathy as a vehicle for social change to gain political power. Sympathy had the power to break the boundaries and divides between the races. White audiences, who wanted to protect their consciences from indictment of moral wrongdoing, did not want to hear the truth over sentimental accounts that idealized Reconstruction race relations. Though sentimental writing was often looked down upon as less serious writing, it commanded large audiences for its entertainment value. A common rhetorical technique employed by Frances Harper and many other African-American writers of the era is the use of sentimentalism as narrative strategy to awake American race consciousness.

The narrator comments on the appearance versus the reality of things in the opening chapter, "Mystery of Market Speech and Prayer-Meeting." In this chapter, the slaves use coded language as resistance. The slaves discuss the Civil War in the coded discourse of mundane activities such as preparing breakfast and other domestic duties. Since whites felt their conversation should be confined to such, disguised speech enables the slaves to communicate safely. "'Did you see de fish in de market dis mornin'? Oh, but dey war splendid, jis' as fresh, as fresh kin be.'"[18] On the surface, it appears to be normal conversation, but Harper helps readers to pay closer attention to decipher the political conversation. "In conveying tidings of the war, if they wished to announce a victory of the Union army, they said the butter was fresh, or that the fish and eggs were in good condition. If defeat befell then, then the butter and other produce were rancid or stale."[19] The slaves invent a language of their own, which enables them to signify upon whites who have oppressed them. Harper's incorporation of black dialect in *Iola Leroy* is a narrative feature of realism. "The distinctiveness of late-nineteenth-century American literature lay largely in the generative role of dialect within it."[20]

The story of *Iola Leroy* is a fictionalized history of slavery, the Civil War, and Reconstruction, but the novel itself contains a series of history lessons applicable to multiple audiences. Other than opening commentary on subtle slave resistance through language, we hear very few details about slavery with the exception of the fact that Iola falls into slavery. Harper's primary focus is placed upon emancipation and Reconstruction. Evidenced by the marital union of Iola and Dr. Latimer, there is a utopian possibility for both racial equality and the restoration of the black community. Exemplary characters, Iola and Dr. Latimer are examples for black men and women to follow in their quests for moral and racial uplift. Harper appeals to the pride of middle- and upper-class blacks in her representations of educated elite black intellectuals. Iola and Dr. Latimer have a primary role of responsibility in developing and uplifting the race.

The narrative is not sequential, and history is not linear. The interjected episodes that disrupt the narrative flow of *Iola* relate the past to the present. There is no apparent chronology to structure coherence throughout *Iola Leroy*. The title character Iola is notably absent from the first six chapters of the novel. Even though Iola appears in Chapter 7, there are two major narrations that interrupt the overall flow of the novel: Dr. Gresham's marriage proposal to Iola and the historical account of Iola's family told in the midst of the narration of the Civil War. These historical interruptions to the narrative flow underscore Iola's life as a part of the Civil War, a major events of our nation's history.

The Civil War sets the stage for the events that occur in *Iola Leroy*, slavery is the fundamental reason why Iola's family has been broken apart and displaced. Iola, raised as a privileged white girl in the antebellum South, is physically white enough to pass. She is the daughter of Eugene Leroy, a white plantation owner, and Marie, a mulatto who is legally Eugene's slave. Iola fits the description of the beautiful tragic mulatta. Early on in the novel, Tom describes Iola: "'My! But she's putty. Beautiful long hair comes way down her back; putty blue eyes, an' jis' ez white ez anybody's in dis place. I'd jis' wish you could see her yoresef.'"[21] Neither Iola nor her two siblings Harry and Gracie know that they are of mixed-race parentage; the children have been protected from finding out their true racial identities. The children believe that they are part of a rich, well-to-do white family. They are educated at the best boarding schools, which provide further protection for their true racial identities.

However, the terrible secret that has been kept from them is revealed when Eugene gets sick, dies, and his racist brother Alfred takes over the state of affairs. Alfred remands Iola and her mother Marie to slavery. Iola's little sister Gracie become the quintessential sentimental tragic mulatto character who swoons and dies upon learning about her black ancestry. She is too weak and too overtaken with shock and grief to live life any longer. Gracie can neither accept her roots nor embrace her history. She rejects the possibility of passing as a solution. Iola succeeds in warning and keeping Harry, who is away at school, safe from the clutches of slavery. Harry has a chance to pass, but he does not. Instead, he chooses not to participate in the white unit of the army, taking a leadership post in the black army instead.

Iola is sold into slavery, but then rescued by Union soldiers. "The General was much impressed by her modest demeanor, and surprised to see the refinement and beauty she possessed."[22] Once again the narrator emphasizes the beauty of the sentimental heroine Iola. The narrator questions, "Could it be possible that this young and beautiful girl had been a chattel, with no power to protect herself from the highest insults that lawless brutality could inflict upon innocent and defenseless womanhood?"[23] The sentiment and emotion evoked from this passage no doubt tugged at the heartstrings of sympathetic white women who could imagine threat to their own virtue. Lurid details of physical abuse perpetuated upon Iola are left out. Iola confesses that she was "tried but not tempted…I was never tempted…I had outrages heaped on me which might well crimson the cheek of honest womanhood with shame."[24] For a sentimental readership, Harper abides by gentility and principles of the cult of true womanhood by telling Iola's life story without specific repulsive details about sexual harassment or physical abuse.

Iola decides to work as a nurse in service to the army. Once Iola finds out that she is part black, she chooses to identify with her black heritage over her white heritage. There are three reasons Iola refuses to marry a white doctor from the North. First, Iola places the need to reunite with her mother and other family members before marrying. Second, Iola tells Dr. Gresham, "There are barriers between us that I cannot pass. Were you to know them I think you would say the same."[25] At this point in the novel, Dr. Gresham is none the wiser that Iola is of mixed-raced heritage. The "barrier" that Iola states cannot be crossed is the "color line." Dr. Gresham is surprised when he learns that Iola is mixed, for she looks as white as he does. "But Iola, ...Your complexion is as fair as mine. What is to hinder you from sharing my Northern home...?"[26] Iola replies, "Were I to marry you I would carry an aching heart into your home and dim its brightness."[27] Despite Iola's misgivings, Dr. Gresham begs for Iola's hand in marriage. "In Iola he saw realized his ideal of the woman whom he was willing to marry. A woman, tender, strong, and courageous, and rescued only by the strong arm of his Government from a fate worse than death."[28] Iola cares for Dr. Gresham and may have actually accepted his marriage proposal if he had said the right thing to her.

Instead, Dr. Gresham says the wrong thing. Dr. Gresham pleads for Iola to deny her racial identity and pass as white forever. Yet Iola's need to fulfill her duty to the racial uplift cause prompts her to deny Dr. Gresham's proposition of marriage. Since Dr. Gresham can only see Iola's visibly white appearance, she asks Dr. Gresham how he would feel about racial atavism: "Doctor, suppose we should marry, and little children in after years should nestle in our arms, and one of them show unmistakable signs of color, would you be satisfied?"[29] A perplexed Dr. Gresham remains speechless, for he "had not taken into account what might result from such a marriage."[30] Dr. Gresham has not considered the possibility of visibly darker black children from their proposed marital union. In her refusal of Dr. Gresham's hand in marriage, Iola also denies privileges of whiteness. Her rejection of Dr. Gresham also solidifies the impossibility of renouncing black heritage. By refusing Dr. Gresham's hand in marriage, Iola also denies privileges of whiteness. Harper's use of sentimental conventions magnifies the realism of

Iola's rejection of Dr. Gresham in favor of the morally right acceptance of her black heritage and racial duty.

Instead of marrying Dr. Gresham, Iola goes off with the mixed-race Robert Johnson to search for her family members. Iola eventually finds her mother and brother Harry to reunite the family. As the novel happily concludes, Iola marries the black Dr. Latimer. Together they nobly devote their lives in service to uplifting the race by promoting education and social activism in an "all black" southern community. Even after she marries, Iola still remains actively employed in the community. Iola's attraction and marriage to Dr. Latimer is not based on sex. "His words were more than a tender strain wooing her to love and happiness, they were a clarion call to a life of high and holy worth, a call which found a response in her heart."[31] Their love is manifested in a higher moral cause of uplifting the black race. Iola's marriage to Dr. Latimer is not consistent with the plot of the romance or sentimental fiction. Their "dawning affections" for one another have their basis in the social cause of black cultural advancement instead of sex or material security.[32] The narrator tells us that "grand and noble purposes" unite Iola and Latimer together.[33]

In the world Frances Harper depicts, Iola and Dr. Latimer are compelled to lead a life in service to the race. They ignore the temptations of Gilded Age society. Gilded Age aesthetics aggrandized the prospect of material wealth versus the social responsibility to serve and lead the black race in pursuit of progress and equality.[34] The title character of *Iola Leroy* emphatically states, "the leader of a race to higher planes of thought and action, to teach men clearer views of life and duty, and to inspire their souls with loftier aims, is a far greater privilege than it is to open the gates of material prosperity and fill every home with serious enjoyment."[35] This passage emphatically states the value of blacks prioritizing service to the race cause. Critical of the Gilded Age social values that Howells privileges in *An Imperative Duty*, Harper criticizes the spirit of progress and prosperity the Gilded Age promotes because combating disenfranchisement and other forms of sociopolitical inequalities is first priority for blacks. The Gilded Age began about 1876 and ended in approximately 1901, marking a time period during which there was a rise of capitalism and great industrial expansion. The Gilded Age illustrated segregation among classes, for the rich became richer, while the poor descended further into poverty.

Harper's perpetuation of "like marrying like" demonstrated by the union of Iola and Dr. Latimer may seem to support the segregationist philosophies of the time period.[36] Seemingly in tandem with the racist separatist politics of the time period, Harper determines that one drop of black blood is enough to prove her protagonist Iola is black. David Hollinger refers to this one-drop rule as "the American practice of treating blackness as a monolithic identity that an individual either has or does not have on the basis of the principle that any African ancestry at all determines that one is simply black."[37] There is no exploration of the possibility of passing for Iola, nor is there discussion of how she will negotiate her partial white heritage. Iola's instant attachment with blackness is rather surprising since she has identified herself as white her entire life. Iola loves Dr. Gresham, but she sacrifices that for a higher cause of moral duty to racial uplift. Iola chooses the love of her "race" over the love of her heart. There is no real indication of romantic love between Iola and Dr. Latimer; they marry because it is the responsible morally right thing to do. *Iola Leroy* could be characterized as a "racial romance" in which the love of "race" replaces the romantic love of a marriage partner. Harper seems to suggest that the more pertinent "race" issues trump matters of the heart.

George W. Stocking notes, "the processes and problems of heredity were little understood, and 'blood' was for many a solvent in which all problems were dissolved and all processes commingled."[38] To some degree, Harper buys into the "one-drop" rule theory, for Iola's blackness negates her whiteness. "One drop of negro blood in her veins curses all the rest."[39] That drop of black blood is drastically different from the white drops of blood that may or may not outnumber the drops of black blood within Iola. This fate Harper prescribes for Iola is consistent with the segregationist philosophies of the time period, which suggested that even one drop of black blood was enough to "taint" a presumed white individual's purity.[40] Yet Harper interprets Iola's black blood as a source of morality over the impure white blood she also possesses. The black blood within Iola determines her character and obligation to moral duty.

Iola's white blood dominates her physical appearance, but appearances are misleading. Iola's physical appearance does not matter, for moral fiber determines the character of her personhood. Iola's rejection of passing "is a fictional strategy that endorses the segregationist's view of racial identity and strictly distinguishes black for white."[41] Passing does not appear to be a viable solution to the problem of the "color line," and Harper reverses the racial value placed upon white versus black blood. Iola's newly discovered black interior and physically white exterior are reconciled only if she adheres to the racial uplift cause and remains true to her moral character. There is no distinction between Iola's racial identity and character, for they are reconciled through conscience, moral fiber, and duty.

Frances Harper places *Iola Leroy*'s climactic moment on the eve of the Civil War. Yet William Dean Howells does not center *An Imperative Duty* within the context of a specific historical event that defines the nation's history. Howells offers an alternate historical perspective on interracial marriage than Harper. *An Imperative Duty* is a historical novel inasmuch as it attempts to narrate the problem of the "color line" within the American scene during the post-Civil War era. Howells did not approve of the sentimental as an appropriate literary vehicle for political assertion. "Not surprisingly, when Howells attempted to write his own realistic version of the novel of passing he placed his characters in situations that would allow them to undermine or reject conventions from the sentimental tradition."[42] Howells adheres to the tenets of realism is in his exploration and criticism of the racial scientific discourse of the time period. However, *An Imperative Duty* ultimately slips into a narrative that is more overtly romantic and idealized. Character is sacrificed over plot, and there is no objective narration in *An Imperative Duty*.

Fiction, for Howells, demanded truth. In his essay "Criticism in Fiction," Howells defined realism as the truthful treatment of material. "The Dean of American Letters" felt compelled to write a "race" novel entitled *An Imperative Duty*, which he published in 1891. Despite his condescending rhetoric, Howells is a complex figure when it comes to race politics. Elsa Nettels argues, "Although he affirmed the unity of mankind, he accepted the widely held belief that race determines temperament and that national or ethnic groups are differentiated by inherited racial traits."[43] Even though Howells questions the racial scientific thought of the term period, his critiques often continue to perpetuate the discourse he interrogates.

The opening chapter of *An Imperative Duty* reads like an ethnographic, journal report where the narrator carefully characterizes Irish immigrants and African-Americans by type of dress, behavior, and lifestyle. Within this opening chapter, the narrator demonstrates his psychological views on racial types and class distinction. Howells establishes Dr. Olney as a narrative authority on the value of black racial character. Dr. Olney observes blacks as subjects that pass as genteel social imitators of white culture and custom. At best, black subjects merely attempt to imitate white ways: "The negroes, if they wished to imitate the manners of our race, wished to imitate the manners of the best among us; they wished to be like ladies and gentlemen."[44] The narrator accepts and perpetuates racial stereotypes. He also expresses concern about the possible threat of black social advancement against white social superiority. The narrator's portrayal of blacks in this passage documents the racial attitudes of the period. Dr. Olney's use of realism's scientific language destroys Howells's realist intention to debunk racial stereotypes. *An Imperative Duty* collapses into a novel that promotes racist thought of the time period.

The novel's opening description of Rhoda foreshadows the revelation of her mixed-race ancestry. Dr. Olney "recalled the particulars of her beauty; her slender height, her rich complexion of olive, with a sort of under-stain of red, and the inky blackness of her eyes and hair."[45] The description of Rhoda's olive skin is consistent with descriptions of mulattos. The mention of an "under-stain of red" foreshadows the issue of "blood" that is central to Rhoda's racial identity.[46] "In Rhoda's features there is a tension between the racially exotic and the classically perfect."[47] The word "blackness" is used to describe Rhoda's eyes and hair. The word "blackness" also metaphorically prescribes Rhoda's sealed fate as potentially tragic. Dr. Olney's overly detailed description of Rhoda's face emphasizes the scientific categorizing of racial attributes. "Her face was of almost classic perfection, and the hair, crinkling away to either temple, grew low upon the forehead, as the hair does in the Clytie head."[48] Dr. Olney describes Rhoda as if she is a specimen for scientific study: "In profile, the mouth was finally accented, with a deep cut outlining, the full lower lip, and a fine just forward of the delicate chin; and the regularity of the mask was farther relieved from insipidity by the sharp wing-like curve in the sides of the sensitive nostrils."[49]

Mrs. Meredith feels that it is her "imperative duty" to reveal the secret of her niece's black heritage once a white minister proposes marriage. Once Rhoda discovers her true racial identity, she immediately writes a letter to the minister who has proposed to let him know that she cannot marry. An upset Rhoda runs off into the night. Mrs. Meredith, sick with grief and worry, overdoses on sleeping pills and dies. Rhoda goes to the "black" side of town to try to achieve a "late-found solidarity of race."[50] She observes the customs of black life to determine whether she can fit into the culture. Part of what ails Rhoda is the fact that blacks in the community fail to take notice of her newly discovered subjectivity. "In the double consciousness of trouble she was as fully aware of everything about her as she was of the world of misery within her."[51] Rhoda possesses a conflicted triple-consciousness, for she is white, black, and then a mixture of both. "There seemed two selves of her, one that lived before that awful knowledge and one that had lived as long since, and again a third that knew and pitied them both."[52] Rhoda lives as a white woman only to discover that she is partially black. Finally, she is neither black nor white. Rhoda is something marginally between the two.

When Dr. Olney first learns of Rhoda's true racial heritage, he is completely repulsed at the fact that she is partially black. "He found himself personally disliking the notion of her having Negro blood in her veins; before he felt pity he felt repulsion."[53] Soon after realizing the stupidity of his prejudice and arrogance, Dr. Olney makes it his "imperative duty" to talk Rhoda out of her depression. "He yearned to take her in his arms and be all the world to one who had no one in all the world."[54] Dr. Olney proposes marriage to Rhoda who has no choice but to accept. Howells rejects sentimental convention; therefore, Rhoda cannot deny Dr. Olney's proposal. Leading a life in service to the black race is the realist prescription that Howells rejects as a solution to Rhoda's racial dilemma.

Rhoda and Dr. Olney's marriage is a representation of the possibility of racial progress. Dr. Olney confesses to Mrs. Meredith, "I've been more and more struck with the fact that sooner or later our race must absorb the colored race; and I believe that it will obliterate not only its color, but its qualities."[55] Dr. Olney's decision to marry Rhoda is based upon his racial theories. Though he accepts Rhoda, Dr. Olney still perceives the white race superior to the black race. "He is willing to let the positive strains ameliorate some of its less desirable tendencies."[56] Dr. Olney's speech demonstrates Howells's vision for mixed-race marriages. Howells believes interracial marriages will provide social equality and evolve the entire human race. Dr. Olney argues, "The way to elevate them is to elevate us, to begin with. It will be an easy matter to deal with those simple-hearted folks after we've got into the right way ourselves."[57] As evidenced by this passage, Dr. Olney believes that whiteness in its superiority will dilute blackness in its inferiority.

Because Dr. Olney buys into scientific Darwinist thought, he is able to look past Rhoda's racial identity to view their union as a model for the evolution of the human race. "Making the novel end in marriage is at least in art a matter of seeing Rhoda's mixture of characters and temperament scientifically enough to make her marriage to a white man evolutionarily sound—and narratively possible."[58] Howells's solution for interracial marriage requires that Dr. Olney and Rhoda live abroad in Italy. Their union neither can sustain itself nor be accepted in America. While the conclusion of the novel concedes to the idea of mixing between the races, there is no acceptable domestic home front for such union.

The "one-drop" rule did not honor mixed racial ancestry as a valid source of racial identification. According to the rule, one drop of black blood negated one's whiteness. In *An Imperative Duty*, Howells asserts that "one drop" of black blood is no different from the drops of white blood Rhoda possesses. Her physical appearance precludes blackness.

Because Rhoda physically appears to be white, it is of no consequence how many drops of black blood she possesses. Dr. Olney argues that Rhoda's racial identification can be determined visually. "For Howells argues in *An Imperative Duty* that appearances are not misleading: in the logic of *An Imperative Duty*, Rhoda's visible whiteness legitimately authorizes her racial whiteness."[59] Dr. Olney maintains that it can never truly be determined how much black blood Rhoda possesses because her physical appearance veils her true racial makeup.

Dr. Olney renounces the segregation logic of hypodescent that defines Rhoda as entirely black. For Dr. Olney, racial identity is something one chooses. Unless Rhoda reveals the truth about her racial identity, those that determine racial identity based on appearance will be fooled into thinking that she is white. The fact that individuals such as Rhoda can choose to pass for white reveals the instability of race as a category of identity. Rhoda embodies the fact that it became increasingly difficult to look at an individual to determine his or her racial origin. The black blood Rhoda possesses is minimal. It can never visually dominate. In *An Imperative Duty* blackness means inferiority, while blackness in *Iola Leroy* is equated with heroism. In Howells's interpretation, Rhoda's white blood possesses the dominant trait, for it determines her physical appearance. Notably, Rhoda does not display any moral "imperative duty" to either race. Ironically, everyone in the novel has an "imperative duty" except Rhoda. Mrs. Meredith feels compelled to reveal Rhoda's true racial ancestry, and Dr. Olney's pity for Rhoda motivates him to provide protection for her through marriage.

Rhoda does not feel compelled to do much of anything initially. She tries to refuse Dr. Olney's proposition for marriage. At his convincing, Rhoda accepts Dr. Olney's hand in marriage and embraces her white ancestry. Howells' rejection of the racial scientific theory of atavism is the reason the marriage between Rhoda and Dr. Olney can occur. Dr. Olney assures Mrs. Meredith, "The natural tendency is all the other way, to the permanent effacement of the inferior type. The child of a white and an octoroon is a sixteenth blood; and the child of that child and a white is a thirty-second blood."[60] Dr. Olney ignores the possibility of Rhoda's black ancestry becoming visible through her children.

He argues, "The chances of atavism, or reversion to the black great-great-great grandfather are so remote that they may be said hardly to exist at all."[61] In his attempt to critique the racial theory of atavism, Howells rejects the possibility of racial inheritance.

Rhoda, unlike Iola, never connects with her black family members. Rhoda does not go through a process of self-realization. Her understanding of race never evolves; it remains stagnant. Whiteness remains the ideal utopia in Howells' *An Imperative Duty*. Therefore, "passing" is the best ending for the novel.[62] Racial passing is the only viable option for Rhoda, who the narrator describes as not very black at all. Metaphorically, Rhoda commits social suicide, for she denies her blackness and rejects her American identity. While Harper clearly articulates that love will not solve the "race problem," Howells tries to present interracial marriage as a possible alternative.[63] Yet Dr. Olney and Rhoda's marital union cannot thrive in America. They go abroad to Italy where their interracial marriage is accepted because of Europe's tolerance for racial difference.

Even though the novel concludes with Dr. Olney and Rhoda's marriage, the two never have children. Dr. Olney and Rhoda are childless, and the possibility of atavism is never fully explored in the novel. Howells designs *An Imperative Duty* as a realist critique of overly melodramatic representations of race and gender. "Howells often disregarded literary sentiment and romance in the promotion of realism."[64] In hopes of avoiding the prescribed tragic death of the stereotyped tragic mulatto, Howells does not let Rhoda die a physical death. Yet her fate is tragic. Rhoda not only fails to embrace her black ancestry on American soil, but she must also hide her true racial identity and embrace a new culture in Italy.

Neither Frances Harper nor William Dean Howells set out to solve or give a literal answer to the "race problem." "So much then, for the question, what is race?"[65] It was too big a problem to present a viable solution. Realism was a subject of controversy in its own time where there were heated debates about whether realism is a suitable mode of representation. Yet Harper and Howells's novels explore the connections between fiction and race in their consideration of how one might best fictionally represent the problem of race. Harper's *Iola Leroy* and Howells's *An Imperative Duty* give two distinctly different fictional representations of race and the "color line." At issue for both novelists is whether black blood can be measured in their mixed-race characters. Harper and Howells use mulatto characters to fictionally represent race in order to criticize the "one-drop" rule. The "one-drop" rule negates the possibility of mixed racial identity because it requires a mixed-race individual's obligation to black racial heritage.

Even though Rhoda is faced with a complex ethical choice, the narrator offers very little portraiture of Rhoda's character interiority and the evolution of her character development. The interracial marital union that Howells imagines between the tragically doomed Rhoda and paternalistic, white savior Dr. Olney can only take place outside an American context. Discussions of marriage seem to take the place of "passing" as a possible solution for Iola and Rhoda's racial dilemmas. Both Iola and Rhoda are faced with the moral and ethical choice of a white versus a black marriage partner. Iola and Rhoda's choices are determined by the racial heritages they pledge allegiance to. Iola chooses to identify with her black heritage. Thus, she chooses to marry her own kind.[66] Rhoda, on the other hand, chooses to identify with her white heritage. Technically, she chooses to marry her own kind as well. Ultimately, Rhoda is not moved by her conscience. Instead, she is moved by her insecurities and selfish desires. Rhoda does not adhere to the calling of "an imperative duty" to participate in the racial uplift cause.

Even though Frances Harper's *Iola Leroy* is rooted in the traditions of the bildungsroman, romance, and sentimental novel, the overarching narration of the text lends to historical realism. Harper intended to write a history, and *Iola Leroy* is a historical novel that covers three time periods: antebellum, Civil War, and Reconstruction. Harper does not allow her character Iola to replicate the tragic mulatto stereotype. Instead, she creates Iola as a historical figure in American history. The novel's focus on Iola's evolving consciousness about race is realist in nature. Like the protagonist of a realist novel, Iola is faced with the complex ethical. She must decide which aspect of her mixed racial identity she will align herself with. The racial identity Iola chooses will determine her choice of marriage partner and racial duty. True to the tenets of a realist novel, the events of *Iola Leroy* are plausible, not sensational or dramatic. Harper depicts reality with an emphasis on verisimilitude. The novel traces Iola's journey from a life rooted in white utopia to a life of black suffering. Iola's journey is complete once she settles into a life defined by black middle-class values. Though Iola is a mulatto heroine, she is neither inherently nor overtly destined to a life of tragedy. Though Iola's life story contains experiences of sexual degradation, Harper abides by the gentility of the sentimental tradition and avoids discussing the lurid details of possible sexual exploitation Iola may have faced. Like the sentimental heroine, Iola avoids the advances of her white suitor Dr. Gresham. She rejects his proposition of marriage and racial passing. Iola is reunited with her family, and her virtue is restored. She marries and lives happily-ever-after. Iola leads a life in service to the racial uplift cause.

At the end of *Iola Leroy*, Frances Harper concludes with a nonfictional, political statement. She admits that she set out to write a text whose threads are made up of both fact and fiction. Harper gives this disclaimer so that *Iola Leroy* will be recognized as historical novel containing truth in its fictive accounts. Harper does not want her novel to be dismissed as romantic. She wants *Iola Leroy* to be recognized as political fiction for social change. Harper aims to prove that *Iola Leroy* is not just a melodramatic romance, but what Claudia Tate terms "an allegory of political desire" that contains "liberational discourses."[67] Tate argues that feminism, romance, and utopian idealism can exist in political narratives about race. The romantic conventions Harper employs in *Iola Leroy* enable her characters to fictionally overcome the obstacles of racism and sexism, which prevent social progress and self-realization.

In *Iola Leroy* social change is fully realized in Harper's utopian vision of a marriage between Iola and Dr. Latimer. Their marriage represents survival, self-reliance, and empowerment in black communities in spite of the politics of slavery and segregation. For Harper, marriage is a metaphorical representation of the racial utopia she remains optimistic about in *Iola Leroy*. Critical of the racist practices of slavery and segregation, Harper envisions an ideal social order characterized by progressive social change. Marriage, an institution of social advancement, can bring about social advancement. Iola and Dr. Latimer's marital union is for the racial uplift cause. As a result, Harper rejects the "storybook" marriage. She promotes a marriage that centers love and passion within the pragmatic, noble, and higher cause of moral duty. Iola and Dr. Latimer's marriage serves as an example of how to build roots and how to sustain a black community. The two join as one by pressing together as social advocates for racial uplift.

On the other hand, William Dean Howells defines marriage as an institution through which the entire human race can progress. In *An Imperative Duty*, the marriage between Rhoda and Dr. Olney serves as an example for the nation to follow. Howells sees interracial marriage as a step in the right direction to solving the race problem. According to Howells, it will serve the greater good of humanity well if the races co-mingle. In his estimation, marriage between blacks and whites will eventually provide a balance instead of a separation between the races. Interracial marriage will evolve the entire race of human beings because it will eventually elevate blackness. Howells's Darwinian thought is evident within his belief that whiteness will not only elevate blackness but also dilute black inferiority. Marriage is the forum for Harper and Howells's critical interpretations of the "one-drop" rule. Iola and Rhoda's moral decisions about which marriage partners they choose metaphorically idealizes the probability of racial harmony in an era socially, culturally, and politically divided by racial tension.

Notes

1. Cathy Boeckmann, *A Question of Character: Scientific Racism and the Genres of American Fiction, 1892–1912* (Tuscaloosa: University of Alabama Press, 2000), 3.
2. *Ibid.*, 3–4.
3. Teresa C. Zackodnik, *The Mulatta and the Politics of Race* (Jackson: University of Mississippi Press, 2004), 25.
4. *Ibid.*, 24.
5. The term "call and response" typically refers to a defining characteristic originating in African music cultural practices, which later became influential to African-American music. In African-American churches call and response typically

refers to the alternation between a leader and chorus. The leader gives a call and the audience responds to the call. This format is also used in the responsive scriptural reading. Call and response is also a trope in African-American literature which refers to intertextuality or conversations across texts. Writers using this technique may or may not know about each other's works.

6. Boeckmann, 13.
7. Zackodnik, 23.
8. Boeckmann, 13–14.
9. Zackodnik, 23.
10. David A. Hollinger, "Amalgamation and Hypodescent: The Question of Ethnoracial Mixture in the History of the United States," *American Historical Review* 108.5 (2003): 1363–1390.
11. *Ibid.*, 1370.
12. Boeckmann, 14.
13. George W. Stocking, "The Turn-of-the-Century Concepts of Race," *Modernism/Modernity*, 1.1 (1994): 6.
14. Hollinger, 1368.
15. Frances E. W. Harper, *Iola Leroy; Or, Shadows Uplifted*, Ed. Hazel V. Carby (Boston: Beacon Press, 1987), 24.
16. Debra Rosenthal, "The White Blackbird: Miscegenation, Genre, and the Tragic Mulatta in Howells, Harper, and the 'Babes of Romance,'" *Nineteenth-Century Literature* 56.4 (2002): 495–517.
17. Claudia Tate, *Domestic Allegories of Political Desire: The Black Heroine's Text at the Turn of the Century* (New York: Oxford University Press, 1992), 147.
18. Harper, 8.
19. *Ibid.*, 9.
20. Gavin Jones, *Strange Talk: The Politics of Dialect Literature in Gilded Age America* (Berkeley: University of California, 1999), 3.
21. Harper, 38.
22. *Ibid.*, 39.
23. *Ibid.*
24. *Ibid.*, 115.
25. *Ibid.*, 109.
26. *Ibid.*, 116.
27. *Ibid.*, 118.
28. *Ibid.*, 59.
29. *Ibid.*, 117.
30. *Ibid.*
31. *Ibid.*, 271.
32. *Ibid.*, 262.
33. *Ibid.*, 271.

34. Kenneth Warren, *Black and White Strangers* (Chicago: University of Chicago Press, 1993), 110.
35. Harper, 219.
36. "Like marrying like" refers to a marriage between two individuals of the same skin color or racial identity. In the case of Latimer and Iola, he is darker skinned and she is of a fair complexion, but they are "like-minded" or devoted to the same principles and causes. In modern day terms, "like marrying like" can refer to marrying someone who is of the same race, educational, religious, or social status.
37. Hollinger, 1368.
38. Stocking, 6.
39. Harper, 67.
40. My use of the word "taint" means to blemish, to stain, or to curse.
41. Kathleen Pfeiffer, *Race Passing and American Individualism* (Amherst: University of Massachusetts Press, 2003), 19.
42. Boeckmann, 142.
43. Elsa Nettels, *Language, Race, and Social Class in Howells's America* (Lexington: University Press of Kentucky, 1988), 87.
44. William Dean Howells, *The Shadow of a Dream and An Imperative Duty*, Ed. Edwin H. Cady (New York: Twayne Publishers, 1962), 141.
45. *Ibid.*, 147.
46. *Ibid.*
47. Boeckmann, 147.
48. Howells, 147.
49. *Ibid.*
50. Howells, 191.
51. *Ibid.*, 193–194.
52. *Ibid.*, 193.
53. *Ibid.*, 165.
54. *Ibid.*, 204.
55. *Ibid.*, 161.
56. Boeckmann, 153.
57. Howells, 229.
58. Boeckmann, 150.
59. Pfeiffer, 56.
60. Howells, 161.
61. *Ibid.*
62. Racial passing, a popular subject-matter in mulatto fiction of the nineteenth-century, refers to an individual whose physical appearance is white but true racial identity is black or mixed-race. Mulattos often have to choose which racial heritage they wanted to align themselves with. The "one-drop" rule and the principle of hypodescent did not allow for a mixed-racial identity. Racial identity fell into

two categories: black or white. There was no grey or mixed shade in between the two extremes. Novels of passing popular during the nineteenth century usually center around a protagonist who must make the morally right choice to either pass as white in order to afford themselves the opportunities that came hand in hand with being white, or to remain true to their black heritage and accept the racism and degradation that came along with being black.

63. The phrase "race problem" refers to the problematic race relations or racial tensions between blacks and whites.
64. Gene Andrew Jarrett, *Deans and Truants: Race and Realism in African American Literature* (Philadelphia: University of Pennsylvania Press, 2007), 43.
65. Stocking, 9.
66. The phrase "own kind" refers to similar racial type, similar racial identification, or someone of the same race.
67. Claudia Tate, *Domestic Allegories of Political Desire: The Black Heroine's Text at the Turn of the Century* (New York: Oxford University Press, 1992), 132.

Chapter 3

Realism, Romance, and Questions of Marital Eligibility in Pauline Hopkins's *Contending Forces* and Edith Wharton's *The House of Mirth*

Marriage has long been valued as an institution where demonstrated commitment between a man and a woman exemplifies one-way society can nurture tradition, morality, and responsibility. Loss of reverence for marriage resulted in not only the decline of American marriage, but also a diminishing of social responsibility. Marriage was a popular subject matter for many realist writers who had hopes of restoring faith in the institution of marriage on an American scene they believed was characterized by moral decline. *Contending Forces* (1900) and *The House of Mirth* (1905), two historical novels, critique Gilded Age social practices. Hopkins's novel satirizes the American nation by showing that the "race problem" is not only a "black" problem, but also a national problem. Hopkins focuses on rape, lynching, and incest to show the profound generational curses blacks and whites have suffered as a result of slavery. By contrast, *The House of Mirth* gives a satirical depiction of the upper-crust New York society to show the tragic suffering that can go on inside an elitist society. While these realist depictions argues that marriage does indeed exemplify the stability, routine, and morality necessary in a healthy social world order, they also reveal that marriage is not fundamentally about romantic love. Marriage and the pursuit of it are central concerns in *Contending Forces* and *The House of Mirth*. These two novels appropriate conventions of realism and romance to show that marriage is not always the ultimate sources of happiness.

Pauline Hopkins's *Contending Forces* and Edith Wharton's *The House of Mirth* demonstrate that making marriage choices has consequences. The female characters in both novels are on the verge of marrying. Dora, Sappho, and Lily are at junctures where they must make marital choices that will have either benefits or costs. Each character is a product of her environment, and each character's marital eligibility is impacted by color and gender prejudices based on white ideals of female beauty. In *Contending Forces*, matrimony equals validation of self and confirmation of virtue for Dora and Sappho, who live in a color-prejudiced world where stereotypes proclaim black women as inferior and sexually compromised. Matrimony equals power and security for *The House of Mirth*'s Lily who exists within a social world that links female whiteness to money, power, and security. What keeps Dora, Sappho, and Lily from rushing into marriage and what motivates Dora and Sappho to marry are central questions that reveal the demands prompted by marriage and standards of female marital eligibility at the-turn-of-the-century.

Marriage functions as a marker of adulthood and social status. Money and respectability are central reasons for marrying. Marriage determines duties and dictates privileges. Confirming patriarchal authority over women, marriage also organizes division of labor and power on the basis of gender. The marital rights of men often exceed those of women, who often suffer silently in marriages replete of love and equality. However, the place of love in marriage changed along with attitudes about race. Realist novels that depict marital difficulties between men and women also moved their focus beyond the demands of the institution of marriage itself. These novels also indict the political and economic institution of marriage itself to show that failed marriages are the result of human and social imperfection. Even though marriage does not facilitate an escape from the gender dictates imposed by the wider society, it is a proper social sphere of interest for women at the turn-into-the-century. Marriage provides a harmonious setting where the possibility of social equality, gender equality, and racial pride exist. Marriage is a key component for directing social progress.

The marriage plot in realist novels usually conforms to one of two types of marriages. The first model suggests that marriage equals happiness and prosperity. This model idealizes the "storybook" marriage, in which the perfect woman and perfect man meet, marry, and live happily-ever-after. This romantic marriage idealizes and promotes possibilities rather than the probabilities of married life. Realist stories such as Charlotte Perkins Gilman's "The Yellow Wall-Paper" (1892) and novels such as Kate Chopin's *The Awakening* (1899) critique this idea of the "storybook" marriage by revealing the consequences of such marital contracts. The consequences include social suicide, death of the individual self, or in some cases, physical death. In this second model, marriage functions as a death sentence imposed upon a protagonist's individual autonomy. Often, this protagonist dies either metaphorically or literally because she is suffocated by an unhappy, loveless, and passionless marriage. Because of the politics of sexual inequality that govern this type of marriage, the protagonist is often forced to publicly submerge her personal identity beneath her husband's identity. Often, the protagonist commits suicide or dies tragically.

Pauline Hopkins uses a combination of traditional romance and domestic realism to explore racial and social themes. Tension between realism and romance is expressed in Hopkins's preface to *Contending Forces*. Hopkins calls and responds to the popular nineteenth-century slave narrative preface. Her preface replicates the rhetorical strategies found in traditional slave narrative prefatory materials. Hopkins's preface incorporates apologia, or the convention of the apology. Hopkins writes, "While I make no apology for my somewhat abrupt and daring adventure within the wide field of romantic literature, I ask the kind indulgence of the generous public for the many crudities which I know appear in the work."[1] A rhetorical strategy in which the slave narrator apologizes in advance for an allegedly mediocre and unpolished work to follow, the apology enables the slave narrator to whittle down the work's level of composition. However, what actually follows the preface is both a rhetorically and politically, well-crafted piece of fiction that defies the expectations of readership. Hopkins finally asks the audience for "their approval of whatever may impress them as being of value to the Negro race and to the world at large."[2]

A novel's romance plot is one that easily engages an audience who understands the language of love and importance of marriage as an institution. Hopkins unites her promiscuous audience through the use of sentiment. *Contending Forces* is dedicated to "the friends of humanity everywhere."[3] Hopkins indicates that she wants to reach a broad audience of readers. Then, she clearly identifies the genre of her novel and her specific reasons for writing. Hopkins states, "In giving this little romance expression in print, I am not actuated by a desire for notoriety or for profit, but to do all that I can in an humble way to raise the stigma of degradation from my race."[4] Hopkins is not writing for money or for pastime. She has written the novel solely on behalf of the racial uplift cause.

Once Hopkins has succeeded in engaging her readers' emotions, the audience is "married" to the romantic plot and its sentimental characters.[5] This contract of sentiment between author and audience provides a rhetorical frame for Hopkins's political address on racial oppression, rape, and lynching. Through fiction, Hopkins generates empathy for factual racial oppression. She defines fiction and its function in her preface: "Fiction is of great value to any people as a preserver of manners and customs—religious, political, and social. It is a record of growth and development from generation to generation."[6] For Hopkins fiction is history made up of both fact and fiction. Hopkins's definition supplies a rationale for her cross-fertilization of realism and romance in the novel. She admonishes African-Americans to write their own fiction and their own histories. Hopkins writes, "*No one will do this for us; we must ourselves develop the men and women who will faithfully portray the inmost thoughts and feelings of the Negro with all the fire and romance which lie dormant in our history.*"[7] Hopkins urges African-American to take responsibility for generating written records to preserve their culture.

The importance of the preface to a work of fiction is almost immeasurable. It provides the author with the opportunity to candidly connect with his or her audience in a way that demonstrates a unique balance between bias and objectivity. Hopkins confesses, "I have tried to tell an impartial story, leaving it to the reader to draw conclusions. I have tried to portray our hard struggles here in the North to obtain a respectable living and a partial education."[8] Hopkins presents her perspective before the reader has the chance to engage with variables of the text, such as narrator, characters, and plot. "I have presented both sides of the dark picture—lynching and concubinage—truthfully and without vituperation, pleading for that justice of heart and mind for my people which the Anglo-Saxon in America never withholds from suffering humanity."[9] The preface itself becomes symbolic of the "contending forces" of fact and fiction. Even though readers take the preface to be a prefatory document of literal truth, the author of the preface often engages in rhetorical play with the audience.

Contending Forces focuses on the American historical realities of slavery, lynching, tabooed interracial marriage, post-Reconstruction disenfranchisement, and job discrimination across several generations of a black family from the pre-Civil War Caribbean to North Carolina, and life in the North. In *Contending Forces,* Pauline Hopkins represents marriage as an act of liberation for black women. Hopkins presents three specific examples of marriage in her novel. One is the secret and tabooed interracial marriage of Charles and Grace Montfort. This marriage is an example of an interracial marriage that is doomed to failure.

The second model of marriage between Dora and Dr. Arthur Lewis shows marriage as a bourgeois social act. Marriage is an expression of black domestic manners and morals of middle- and upper-class social standing. This type of marriage is primarily based upon respect. Dora respects and wants to join the race-cause that Dr. Lewis has undertaken. Dora and Dr. Lewis respect each other first, and then they come to love each other. This couple's love is based upon a mutual commitment to advance the racial uplift cause. Their dedication to the race cause demonstrates their level of commitment to each other. Their marriage also functions as an example of how black men and women should join together in matrimony. Hopkins asserts that the foundation of a successful black marriage is work and spiritual partnership.

The third model of marriage between Sappho and Will Smith is based upon mutual passion and desire. Hopkins obliterates the stereotype of the black woman as wanton and licentious by sanctioning Sappho's monogamous desire for Will through the institution of marriage. Hopkins emphasizes that Sappho's desire is not forced or coerced upon her in the form of rape, prostitution, or a stereotypical exotic-primitive nature. Instead, Sappho's desire originates within herself. Her virtue and purity are restored through the act of marriage. Sappho and Will's desire for one another is acceptable because it is rightfully expressed as husband and wife.

The story of *Contending Forces* is a frame within a frame. The opening story of the Montforts during the 1790s frames the larger story of the romantic plot between Sappho Clark and Will Smith. This pre-Emancipation plot history serves as a retrospect of the past. It demonstrates that the present repeats the past and the past actively informs the present. The opening historical account focuses on a slaveholder from Bermuda named Charles Montfort, who "was neither a cruel man, nor an avaricious one."[10] Montfort's wife, Grace, is rumored to have black blood coursing through her veins. She is described as "a dream of beauty even among beautiful women."[11] Descriptions of her exotic and mysterious beauty contain clear racial overtones regarding her physical appearance: "Tall and slender; her form was willowy, although perfectly molded. Her complexion was creamy in its whiteness, of the tint of the camellia; her hair, a rich golden brown, fell in rippling masses far below the waist line."[12] Despite the fact that she is "a most lovely type of Southern beauty," Grace is stripped and raped.[13] Tied to a post, Grace is whipped by the overseers of Anson Pollock, an evil slave master in the community.

White but powerless, Charles Montfort is unable to protect his wife. Grace's symbolic fall from the "grace" of whiteness to the infamy of blackness is emphasized by the vivid frontispiece portrait of her lying in a pool of black blood at the feet of two white men. Grace's alleged black blood oozes out of her "white tender back."[14] This visual representation of blood serves as a literal warning of reminder that white women are vulnerable to sexual violence. There is no physical protection in marriage for Grace. Stripped of her whiteness, Grace becomes black without any change in her racial composition. Loss of whiteness is a theme throughout *Contending Forces.*

Critical of pervading theories of inherited "racial taint" and notions of "tainted blood," Hopkins critiques the notion that racial essences are transmitted through biological inheritance.[15] The following passage is an example where "blood" does not mean "character": "In many cases African blood had become diluted from amalgamation with the higher race, and many of these 'colored' people became rich planters or business men (themselves owning slaves) through the favors heaped upon them by their white parents."[16] Hopkins manipulates racial signifiers by giving words such as "nature," "blood," and "character" difficult and inconsistent meanings to negate theories of racial determinism. She highlights the precarious nature of racial classification. *Contending Forces* never reveals the true racial identity of the Montforts despite all the rumors and accusations: "This being the case, there might even have been a strain of African blood polluting the fair stream of Montfort's vitality, or even his wife's, which fact would not have caused him one instant's uneasiness."[17] In her appropriation of the discourse of "blood tainting," it may appear that Hopkins supports the racial myth that white blood is superior to black blood. However, Hopkins reverses the values of positive character to black blood and negative character to white blood. The narrator does hint that there is some possible truth to the rumor about the Montforts' racial identities precisely because there is no such thing as "pure blood" or a "pure race."[18]

Charles Montfort's racial identification neither shields him from being stripped of social power nor prevents him from losing his life. Both Charles and Grace's dispossession of whiteness reveals the socially constructed nature of racial categories. Though Grace and Charles Montfort love each other, love is not enough. Their interracial union is dishonored and unaccepted. The Montforts are resigned to a fate of death. Hopkins appears to suggest that interracial marriages are doomed to death. The tragic story of the Montforts frames the central story of Jesse's grandchildren, Will and Dora Smith.

Will and his sister Dora assist their mother in running a family-owned boarding house. Sappho Clark and John Langley room in the boarding house. Will falls in love with Sappho, an extremely beautiful mulatto woman who possesses a mysterious Southern past. Even though John Langley is engaged to Dora, he lusts after Sappho. John Langley's intentions with Sappho are dishonest, for he wants Sappho to be his mistress. To escape John, Sappho leaves town. She leaves a letter for Will, her one true love. Sappho explains her mysterious and tragic past of rape, forced prostitution, and single motherhood. Will shares the incriminating information about John with Dora. Upon discovering John's true character, Dora immediately breaks off their engagement. Dora eventually marries Dr. Arthur Lewis, her former childhood friend who heads a large industrial school for blacks in Louisiana. While visiting Dora and her new husband, Will unexpectedly runs into Sappho. A few weeks later, the two marry. The moral of the story suggests that virtuous black women are rewarded with happy marriages. Furthermore, they manifest their love for their husbands through dedication to moral uplift and racial progress.

Sappho Clark is the premier heroine of *Contending Forces*, but Dora Smith's story shadows Sappho's story. Sappho is an attractive, unmarried mulatto woman whose goal is to be approved by the black middle-class and restored to that community. Dora is fascinated by Sappho's beauty. She describes Sappho as a "woman with a story written on her face."[19] Sappho desperately wants to overcome the trauma of her past, so that she may succeed at achieving true womanhood. As the story reveals, Sappho is indeed a survivor, but the emotional and psychological effects of her past threaten her new identity and place within the black community. Many of Sappho's flaws are not her own fault. As a consequence of slavery's institutional practices, Sappho is raped, forced into prostitution, and unwillingly pushed into motherhood.

Dora desires an intimate friendship with Sappho even though she "did not as a rule, care much for girl friendship, holding that a close intimacy between two of the same sex was more than likely to end disastrously for one or the other."[20] Pauline Hopkins appears to suggest that before women can enter into meaningful marital relationships, there must be solidarity between women. Bonds between women solidify and secure meaningful alliances between men and women in marriage. Dora considers Sappho a mentor, so she confides in Sappho about her engagement and future plans with John Langley. Many of Pauline Hopkins's philosophies about marriage surface through dialogue between Dora and Sappho.

Sappho defines the importance of love in the following passage: "I think you will be happy, Dora, if you love him. All things are possible if love is the foundation stone."[21] For Hopkins, love has a definite place in marriage. Happiness in a marriage can only occur if there is love. Dora does not love her fiancé John. She states, "I like him well enough to marry him, but I don't believe there's enough sentiment in me to make love a great passion, such as we read of in books."[22] Dora's judgment is not clouded by the fairytale love depicted in romance novels. Love is the foundation of a marriage, and a marriage without love creates a miserable existence for a woman. Marriage fiction is often instructional for women readers aspiring to marry.

Dora understands the difference between romantic possibilities and realistic probabilities in matrimony. She believes that love has absolutely nothing to do with marriage because people marry for the practical reasons of compatibility and tolerance. Dora likes John well enough such that she can stand to marry him. She believes that she can tolerate John in marriage. Dora's negative outlook on marriage reflects her fear that she will get tired of John. Sappho explains to Dora, "It is generally the other way: the men get tired of us first. A woman loves one man, and is true to him through all eternity."[23] Sappho's insights clearly reflect prevalent gender roles and gender stereotypes associated with marriage. Dora likes John for a superficial reason, his physical appearance. John is a handsome man and jealous community women desire him. However, it is foreshadowed that a marriage between Dora and John will fail. John is a descendant of Anson Pollock, the villainous murderer of Dora's ancestors narrated in the earlier part of the novel.

Dr. Arthur Lewis is Dora's second choice of a marriage partner. After her depressing outlook on marriage to John, Dora talks to Sappho about Dr. Lewis. Dr. Lewis is Dora's childhood friend who has become a successful scholar and businessman. Sappho states, "If I didn't know but that he might be the mysterious link which join love, marriage, and the necessary man in a harmonious whole."[24] It is clear that Dora loves Dr. Lewis, and that he is a better love match than John. Dr. Lewis encompasses everything Dora desires in a mate. Dora admires his work on behalf of the racial uplift cause, and the novel forecasts that the two will unite because of their love for the black race.

Dora questions Sappho, "Do you believe marriage is the beautiful state it is painted by writers?"[25] Sappho feels uncomfortable discussing marriage because she feels unworthy of marriage. The narrator makes it clear that concealing the past is one of the potential character flaws that could possibly threaten Sappho's restored identity. Sappho, though a mulatto character, is not depicted as inherently tragic. Mrs. Willis from the sewing circle states, "I would not worry about the fate of the mulatto, for the fate of the mulatto will be the fate of the entire race. It is an incontrovertible truth that there is no such thing as an unmixed black on the American continent."[26] This quote clearly articulates that Hopkins incorporated mulatto characters as symbolic representation of the connections between the segregated races. Mrs. Willis believes that all blacks are of mixed-race descent, and slavery is to blame for the prevalent interracialism. Further, Mrs. Willis believes the advancement and uplift of the race depends upon black women.

The sewing circle symbolizes black women's clubs popular to the late nineteenth century. Mrs. Willis, the mulatto woman who presides over the sewing circle meeting, has taken upon herself the task of guiding the younger black women of the community. "The best opening she decided, she decided after looking carefully about her, was in the great cause of the evolution of true womanhood in the work of the 'Woman Question' as embodied in marriage and suffrage."[27] As a more experienced lady, Mrs. Willis knows that she bears a responsibility to younger women of the community. The future of the race depends upon them. Sappho, a member of the circle, surrounds herself with black women who share interest in racial uplift and marriage. Mrs. Willis teaches the young women at the sewing circle about "the place which the virtuous woman occupies in upbuilding a race."[28] She teaches the young women that they are responsible for speaking out and on behalf of women's rights. "Woman questions" such as marriage and motherhood never have to take a back seat to the larger race cause.[29]

A major question in *Contending Forces* is whether Sappho meets female standards of marriageability. Sappho's tragic past suggests that she is unlikely to marry and achieve the happily-ever-after coveted by many women. Traditional standards of female virtue promoted virginity as a primary indicator of female virtue and marital eligibility. Though rape, unwed motherhood, and prostitution are tangible identifications that Sappho's virtue has been compromised, Mrs. Willis defines virtue as, "'Strength to do the right thing under all temptations.'"[30] Mrs. Willis offers a definition of virtue that takes a different approach to nineteenth-century criteria for the cult of true womanhood.[31] Mrs. Willis defines virtue as the ability of young black women to make sound ethical decisions that reflect their strong moral character. Mrs. Willis suggests that traditional cult of true womanhood "ideas of virtue are too narrow."[32] Defining virtue solely in relation to the physical body overlooks equally important choices women must make concerning their minds, emotions, and spirituality.

Sappho is faced with the proposition of at least three marriage proposals. Enamored by Sappho's beauty, Will asks for Sappho's hand in marriage. Sappho loves Will, but she believes he will reconsider his marriage proposal once he learns about her past. As a result, Sappho rejects Will's marriage proposal and runs away to escape the shame of her past. The remainder of the novel's story focuses on Sappho's virtue and marital eligibility. In attempts to overcome the trauma of her past, Sappho wants to be approved by the black middle-class and restored to the community. Acknowledging and reclaiming her abandoned son is the only way she can emerge from the shame of rape and unwed motherhood.

Sappho makes the virtuous choice to commit her future life to building a relationship with her son, Alphonse. She also makes the virtuous choice to reject the marriage proposition by Monsieur Louis, her employer. Though Monsieur Louis's proposal is a viable means for Sappho to restore her pride and virtue, Will Smith finds and reunites with Sappho just in time. Once Will and Sappho reunite, they tell Monsieur Louis their stories. He responds, "It is indeed a fairy tale of love and chivalry such as we read of only in books…happy love—a love sanctified and purified by suffering."[33] As the story concludes, Sappho is an example of a woman whose physical virtue is violated but restored.

The obstacles that initially prevent Sappho and Will from being together do not stifle the happily-ever-after outcome of their love. *Contending Forces* is a romance about love and desire sanctioned through marriage. The novel contains a romantic marriage plot even though the novel presents a realist discourse about female standards of marital eligibility. The "storybook" marriage is attainable for the physically beautiful mulatto character Sappho despite assaults upon her virtue and threatened exposure of her troubled past. Pauline Hopkins rewrites the script for the stereotyped tragic mulatto character through Sappho Clark. Sappho is mulatto, but Hopkins demonstrates that mulattos are not inherently tragic. To the contrary, Sappho successfully marries the man of her dreams and takes a respectable place in the black community. Even a mulatto woman with a traumatic past can have a fairytale, happily-ever-after ending.

This happily-ever-after moral to the story calls to mind the fact that marriage and motherhood were social roles that were denied as a result of the cruel practices of slavery. Hopkins shows the progression of increased marriage rights and marital eligibility for African-American women at the turn-of-the-century. Slave marriages often went unrecognized by white slaveholders. In some instances, slave masters picked who their slaves would marry. In cases where slaves had chosen their own mates, masters often spitefully separated husbands and wives. Under the cruel practices of slavery, slaves did not possess the civil right of marriage. Yet in spite of the circumstances surrounding their lack of civil liberties, many slaves found ways to sanction their own marriages as legal and spiritual bonds in the sight of God.

Distinguishing between marriage under slavery and its legacy after emancipation is essential. After emancipation, marriage for African-Americans was an expression of self-agency and an announcement of self-authority. For this reason, the marriage plot of love and courtship appealed to African-American women writers who used it for the expressed purpose of presenting arguments for social reform. Sentimental and romance narrative forms assisted African-American women writers in engaging popular audiences' sympathies in order to inoffensively educate potentially resistant audiences to generate empathy for racial oppression. In *Domestic Allegories of Political Desire,* Claudia Tate argues that idealized marriage plots depicted more than happiness and prosperity in African-American women's sentimental and romance narratives.[34]

Tate argues that these idealized marriage plots are actually "domestic allegories of political desire" about dreams of freedom, equality, and civil liberty that newly emancipated blacks had.[35] Marriage is a literal representation of liberation. It is a new civil right, which confirms the legal status of a black person. Many black women exercise the choice of remaining single or postponing marriage to pursue careers in business, as marriage often impose limitations on their public personas and professional work. Pauline Hopkins's *Contending Forces* represents marriage as an act of liberation that confirms a black individual's ex-slave status. This definition of marriage as a social relation is evident in two seemingly unlikely texts in conversation, *Contending Forces* and *The House of Mirth.*

The intricate connection between race and class in realist and romance narratives is evident through Pauline Hopkins and Edith Wharton's appropriation of the language of "blood" in their modern discourses on marriage. Popular notions of class had their origins in racist views of "blood" as a metaphor for race. Social behaviors and biologically inherent characteristics were often associated with blood. For example, Pauline Hopkins uses the term "cracker blood" to explain John Langley's villainous behavior in *Contending Forces*[36] Yet in *The House of Mirth,* Edith Wharton often refers to blood as an indicator of a character's class standing, and the novel seeks to determine whether class is inherited or essential like race. Wharton uses skin color and associates it with class characteristics. For example, Gus Trenor, arguably the villain of the novel, is described "with a reddening brow" and a "face darkened to rage."[37] Lower class characters are described as having darker complexions and features. In *The House of Mirth*, Edith Wharton often refers to "blood" as an indicator of a character's social refinement. Lily is caught in a class struggle and the novel seeks to determine whether class is inherited or essential like race.

Class was defined on an evolutionary chain of being, and realist novels often accommodate the interests and aspirations of an insurgent middle class. Edith Wharton's *The House of Mirth* presents conflict and confrontation between the inherently wealthy upper class and lower class. Wharton appropriates Darwinian theories of culture to criticize the upper class of Old New York society that is responsible for the protagonist Lily's social downfall. As Lily gradually descends from high to low class life, it becomes apparent that class standing determines who is fittest to survive. Lily's descending class status is the reason she fails to survive. Wharton identifies money and manners as inherited traits that the high society deteriorates from.

Lily Bart, an attractive, naïve, and unmarried young woman, has as her primary goal to be married to a wealthy man. In addition, she seeks the approval of the rich upper-class society that she so desperately wants to be a part of. Lily has a number of self-imposed tragic flaws: gambling, naiveté, greed, and obsession with class standing. Lily's obsession with wealth and prestige cause her to make poor decisions. For example, Lily foolishly rejects Selden's marriage proposal because he does not possess enough money according to her social standards. Her judgment of Selden's financial insecurity ironically contrasts with her own lack of wealth to attract a husband and secure her own future. Lily is enslaved to the social demands of the upper class society, but she descends into abject loneliness and poverty.

In *The House of Mirth* marriage determines social progress and a woman's class status. In her realistic depictions of the demands prompted by marriage and portraits of married life, Edith Wharton refuses to allow her novel to bow to the conventions of the romance characterized by happy endings. Instead, the novel adheres to the conventions of realism, depicting the suicide of Lily Bart. "Coding race as a class attribute, Wharton was able to turn her gaze on the upper classes—the group she famously called 'a frivolous society'—through the use of realism's tools."[38] Wharton writes about class issues in racial terms. Lily's white body becomes an emblem of her class status. Loss of whiteness, a clear theme in *The House of Mirth*, highlights the symbiotic relationship between race and class. As Lily gradually descends from high society to the lower classes of society, she also "loses" her whiteness.[39] Wharton highlights this because she considered realism "unfairly appropriated for the representation of the lower classes."[40] White women such as Lily are socially vulnerable and physically unprotected when class standing is the criteria for their survival rate.

Edith Wharton's *The House of Mirth* explores the consequences that coveted social class mobility and material wealth have upon its protagonist, Lily Bart. In the novel, the house is a representation of an elite social class or social network. Yet there is no "mirth" in the social network Wharton depicts.[41] Instead, the novel presents a very grim tale of a society that rejects a poor young woman who aspires toward high social class standing. "Society did not turn away from her, it simply drifted by, preoccupied and inattentive, letting her feel, to the full measure of her humbled pride, how completely she had been the creature of its favor."[42] The "house" in the title seems to accurately represent a miserable class of people. No one is truly happy within this upper-crust society that Lily desperately wants to be a part of. Those who secure their financial and social position within upper-class society masquerade around as if they are happy. The material wealth and prestige that being a part of this upper-class affords is not a guarantor of happiness.

Lily's beauty and socioeconomic status are factors in determining whom she will marry. Ironically, a lily is a flower that represents purity. Read through a discourse of class, Lily does not live up to her name's definition of purity. Lily is a divided and conflicted individual who does not securely fit into any appropriate class; however, she has been violated by the experience of rejection from both classes. *The House of Mirth* debates about the proper place for Lily in a society where the social effects of not marrying generate problems for existence and conformity within a society that shuns unmarried women. Lily expresses her frustration: "I have tried hard—but life is difficult, and I am a very useless person. I can hardly be said to have an independent existence. I was just a screw of a cog in the great machine I called life, and when I dropped out of it I found I was of no use anywhere else."[43] The "great machine of life" is a metaphorical representation for the upper-class society that Lily covets membership within.

The extent to which Lily comes to understand the manners of proper and improper social behavior determines her viability in upper-class society. In her portrayal of manners, Wharton reveals that some manners are common knowledge "social drudgery" that must be performed.[44] Other manners are secret knowledge that only certain individuals are privy to. The manners the elite class members artificially display are a façade for the bad manners, lying, cheating, stealing, adultery, and gossiping, which they perform. Lily recognizes the superficiality of these manners, which members of the elite class perform to mask their ugly manners: "It was no longer, however, from the vision of material poverty that she turned with the greatest shrinking. She had a sense of deeper impoverishment—of an inner destitution compared to which outward conditions dwindled into insignificance."[45] In this passage, Wharton emphasizes Lily's long delayed recognition of the importance of moral character over material wealth. As Lily slips into abject poverty, she becomes ashamed that she has obsessively pursued superficial upper-class values.

Selden, a potential marriage partner, knows "the real Lily."[46] Selden understands that beauty is a key part of Lily's tragic existence on both the marriage and social class markets. His physical descriptions of Lily's beauty conform to descriptions of the popular racial science. Yet Selden fears Lily's beauty, for it has the power to attract and even destroy him. Selden is the only character in the novel that is truly happy. He is happy because he is socially mobile within the elite social circles. Selden knows how to detach himself as an outside observer from the superficial and material aspects of high society. He is socially equipped, for he is able to adapt to situations without compromising his moral ideals and principles.

Selden is also the only character in the novel that truly understands Lily inside and out. "In the long moment before the curtain fell, he had time to feel the whole tragedy of her life."[47] Before Lily dies, Selden is aware of the tragedy in her beauty. "It was as though her beauty, thus detached from all that had cheapened and vulgarized it, had held out suppliant hands to him from the world in which he and she had once met for a moment, and where he felt and overmastering longing to be with her again."[48] Selden recognizes that Lily wants to be saved. If he can convince Lily to marry him, Selden knows that he can save her from an impending demise. Even though Lily's true love is Selden, she bypasses numerous opportunities to marry him. According to Lily's standards, Selden does not have enough money. As a result, she foregoes numerous opportunities to unite in holy matrimony with him. Ironically, Lily has very little money herself, but she gambles with love. Lily is tragically enslaved to the impossibility of being happy without wealth and social status. Selden, the only character in the novel that is truly happy, is able to do what Lily cannot. He moves within the elite social circles, but he manages to detach himself from the trappings of high society.

Simon Rosedale, the other gentleman in love with Lily, is a Jew. He delights in Lily's "gestures of coquetry."[49] Rosedale understands that Lily's beauty is part of her tragic existence, but he also understands that Lily's betwixt and between social status is the root cause of discrimination leveled against her. As a Jew, Rosedale understands what it means to exist on the margins of society. Rosedale fears Lily's beauty it contains the dangerous power that can facilitate her survival in an unsuitable class environment. Lily's consideration of Rosedale as a candidate for marriage further indicates that she is desperately willing to take the chances of further descending down the social ladder to secure wealth and marriage. A racially mixed marriage between Rosedale and Lily would be social suicide.

The rumor of Lily's affair with Bertha Dorset's husband gets Lily expunged from high society forever. It also destroys any possibility of marriage for Lily. The narrator questions, "What debt did she owe to a social order which had condemned and banished her without trial?"[50]

There is no trial. In addition to the charges of adultery, Lily becomes an outcast of society due to the fact that she lacks a husband and money. Lily tries to go through a "social rehabilitation," in attempt to repair her social reputation, but "she had fallen, she had "gone under."[51] Lily fails to socially rehabilitate herself, and she descends deeper into poverty and seclusion from the upper-social world she covets. "The ever-revolving wheels of the great social machine" continue spinning despite Lily's bad fortune.[52] Fate in the form of bad luck seems to be working against Lily.

Popular social Darwinist thought informs Edith Wharton's presentation of Lily's social behavior and its resulting social consequences. Wharton incorporates this notion of fate with popular social Darwinist theories. Lily "was beginning to have fits of angry rebellion against fate, when she longed to drop out of the race and make an independent life for herself. But what manners of life would it be?"[53] According to social Darwinist thought, only the fittest survive and the unfit are doomed to extinction. Lily is neither fit for society nor fit for marriage. Only some members of society are cut out for success. Clearly, Lily is not one who will achieve social standing through marriage. She is doomed to failure in a world where only some members of society are cut out for success. Lily recognizes her impending doom and commits suicide. When Selden shows up the following day to propose marriage, he is too late. "But at least he *had* loved her."[54] Selden understands the tragedy of Lily's death and their unrequited love as something beyond human control. Social forces and conditions beyond their control "conspired to keep them apart."[55]

Joan Lidoff argues that *The House of Mirth* "is primarily a romance of identity."[56] Lily's death by suicide is a tragic romance ending, but it is also an appropriate ending for a realist novel with a discourse of modern marriage. Instead of a marriage at the end of a romance novel, a tragic death concludes *The House of Mirth*. The novel's biting realism reveals the conflict between idealized notions of marriage and probable standards of marital eligibility. The moral of the story appears to be that happiness cannot be bought, and no amount of wealth equates with the value of happiness. Lily refused the possibility of marital bliss in Lawrence Selden because he did not measure up to the social and monetary standards that she so tragically coveted until her death.

Comparatively, there are some striking similarities and differences between Lily and Sappho's journeys to finding true happiness and love. Illicit advances are made to Lily and Sappho by villainous male characters. In *The House of Mirth,* the married Gus Trenor makes illicit advances toward Lily. Gus Trenor schemes to make Lily indebted to him both financially and physically as his mistress. In *Contending Forces,* an engaged and nearly married John Langley makes illicit advances toward Sappho. He attempts to blackmail Sappho into becoming his mistress in order to secure the secrets of her past. Both Lily and Sappho are objects of sexual interest and potential sexual exploitation desperately trying to establish their virtue and marital eligibility. On the verge of marrying, these women strive to defend their reputations as single women with aspirations toward marital security.

In *The House of Mirth,* the "storybook" marriage is unattainable despite the protagonist Lily's beauty. Edith Wharton's *The House of Mirth* clearly argues that love and death are the two safest states of being for a woman. Lily has several opportunities to seize love and find happiness, but she is blinded by her obsession for wealth and luxury. Since Lily chooses not to experience true happiness in love, death is the only possible means for her redemption. In *The House of Mirth,* Lily tragically dies of unrequited love after being cast out of upper-class society. She must suffer the consequences of social ostracism because she is unmarried and improperly established within society. Lily exists on the margins of society, and the ultimate consequence of her transgression against the social order is death.

In both *Contending Forces* and *The House of Mirth,* marriage becomes the metaphor for social progress. In *Contending Forces,* marriage is presented as a means of both individual and racial advancement over oppression. Similarly, in *The House of Mirth,* marriage is presented as a means of personal material gain and social climbing. The stories of *Contending Forces* and *The House of Mirth* express anxiety about social changes taking place at the turn-of-the-century that may be described as "cultural amalgamation."[57] Sappho Clark and Lily Bart are caught in class struggles whose outcomes raise questions about whether race, class, and gender identity are inherited, constructed, or essential categories of difference.

Lily and Sappho's impending choices about marriage predict whether they will survive the cruelties society can perpetuate on black and white women. Two historical novels, *The House of Mirth* and *Contending Forces* demonstrate how race and gender are related by showing that gender is more concrete of a category than race. Particularly in relation to women's issues, gender is more solid than race. Both Wharton and Hopkins describe the particular and unconscionable prescribed relationship women had to beauty. Sappho states it best: "Men call me beautiful...what has beauty been to me but a curse?"[58] Beauty truly comes in the form of a curse to both Lily and Sappho. Women who were meant to become beautiful objects had as their only responsibility to embody beauty. As supreme and artistic perfections, these women had to marry well. Both Sappho Clark and Lily Bart are extremely beautiful women. Their auras captivate men, but their beauty is duped. Lily "liked to think of her beauty as power for good, as giving her the opportunity to attain a position where she should make her influence felt in the vague diffusion of refinement and good taste."[59] Sappho is described as a "girl, resembling nothing so much as a lily in its beautiful purity."[60] Motivated by socioeconomic status, standards of white beauty function as both social capital and commodity according to the culture and taste that dictate society's capacity to appreciate and exploit Lily and Sappho's beauty. For it is at the expense of beauty that Lily and Sappho are duped by society's forced expectations upon them as women who must marry.

Notes

1. Pauline Hopkins, *Contending Forces*, Ed. Henry Louis Gates, Jr. (New York: Oxford University Press, 1988), 13.
2. *Ibid.*
3. *Ibid.*, 7.
4. *Ibid.*, 13.
5. My use of the word "married" means joined to, committed to, or engaged within.

6. Hopkins, 13–14.
7. *Ibid.*, 14.
8. *Ibid.*, 15.
9. *Ibid.*
10. *Ibid.*, 22.
11. *Ibid.*, 40.
12. *Ibid.*
13. *Ibid.*
14. *Ibid.*, 69.
15. The word "taint" means blemished or stained. If "blood" is tainted it's "bad blood" or flawed blood. These kinds of racial terms and meanings were popular during the late-nineteenth-century era of racial scientific thought.
16. Hopkins, 23.
17. *Ibid.*
18. According to the racial scientific discourse on "blood," pure means untainted or unstained by racial blemish. "Pure blood" and "pure race" are terms applied to whiteness or white racial identity.
19. Hopkins, 89.
20. *Ibid.*, 97–98.
21. Hopkins, 118.
22. *Ibid.*, 119.
23. *Ibid.*, 122.
24. *Ibid.*, 123.
25. *Ibid.*, 119.
26. *Ibid.*, 151.
27. *Ibid.*, 146.
28. *Ibid.*, 148.
29. Many black women activists of the nineteenth-century highlighted the tension between the "race problem" and "woman questions." Many of these women did not want to put black women's rights issues on the back-burner to focus on larger "race" concerns. Racial uplift was important but so were black women's rights.
30. Hopkins, 149.
31. The cult of true womanhood was primarily a nineteenth-century set of ideologies which promoted white women's dedication to virtue, piety, purity, chastity, and domesticity. Narratives of nineteenth-century black women writers such as Harriet Jacobs and Frances Harper often asserted that black women defined and subscribed to their own tenets of female virtue.
32. Hopkins, 149.
33. Hopkins, 398.
34. Claudia Tate, *Domestic Allegories of Political Desire: The Black Heroine's Text at the Turn of the Century* (New York: Oxford University Press, 1982), 11–12.

35. *Ibid.*, 2.
36. Hopkins, 221.
37. Edith Wharton, *The House of Mirth* (New York: The Modern Library, 1999), 144–145.
38. Augusta Rohrbach, *Truth Stranger Than Fiction: Race, Realism, and the U. S. Literary Marketplace* (New York: Palgrave, 2002), 100.
39. The fact that this character can "lose" her racial composition points to the fallibility of the racial scientific discourse of the late-nineteenth-century and the instability of racial categories.
40. Rohrbach, 100.
41. The word "mirth" means gaiety or merriment.
42. Wharton, 257.
43. *Ibid.*, 303.
44. *Ibid.*, 39.
45. *Ibid.*, 313.
46. *Ibid.*, 149.
47. *Ibid.*, 133.
48. *Ibid.*, 133–134.
49. *Ibid.*, 71.
50. *Ibid.*, 295.
51. *Ibid.*, 281.
52. *Ibid.*, 258.
53. *Ibid.*, 38.
54. *Ibid.*, 324.
55. *Ibid.*
56. Joan Lidoff, "Another Sleeping Beauty: Narcissism in The House of Mirth," *American Realism: New Essays*, Ed. Eric J. Sundquist (Baltimore: Johns Hopkins University Press, 1982), 239.
57. Rohrbach, 106.
58. Hopkins, 321.
59. Wharton, 34.
60. Hopkins, 115–116.

Conclusion

Realist Delineations of Married Life

In the preceding chapters, I have directed attention to social standards of marriage and the ranges of resulting marital behaviors among protagonists in selected novels of the realist period. I have used depictions of marriage's moral currency and political economy to demonstrate both the enticing prospects and disdain for American marriage during the Age of Realism. Many realist writers felt that marriage could restore morality to the American nation characterized by race and gender tensions, the evolution of capitalism, and industrialism and market exchange. One conclusion I have drawn is that some realist novels often romanticize the relation of marriage. Frances Smith Foster's *Love and Marriage in Early African America* "begins with the ideal—the concept of love, the initial ideas and desires that many of us have when our attraction to others has moved from pestering or playing games to looking for love, or being "In Love—with Love" in her opening discussion of the of the romanticization of the marriage plot.[1] Foster asserts, "Back in the day, whether to marry was not a very serious concern. Marriage was considered a good thing for the community, and generally, a good thing for a particular individual."[2] Therefore, whether to marry or not was not so much an important concern as the act of choosing one's mate wisely. For this reason, romantic love may or may not have played as pivotal a role in the selection of a marriage partner. "Romantic love may be the proper prelude to marriage, but more important is the social foundation it establishes."[3] Yet, the sequence that "love should beget marriage, marriages should make families, and families should and do form the bedrock of civilization" remains an American tradition, both past and present.[4]

In *Black and White Strangers*, Kenneth Warren argues, "It was long held that American realism's failures both political and aesthetic resulted from the stranglehold of sentimental and romantic forms on the American imagination."[5] Though these novels contain marriage plots, love and marriage may not be the central focus. This tension is evidenced by romantic idealization versus characters in realist novels struggling to confront issues of moral and social significance. While realist characters are considered products of their own environments, sentimental and romantic characters are thought to be products of their excessive feelings. That *Megda, An Imperative Duty, Iola Leroy, The Awakening, Contending Forces*, and *The House of Mirth* draw on features of sentimental and romantic conventions enables them to critique marriage, challenge sexist gender representations, and debunk racist characterizations. Such novels contain "excessive features of sentimental writing that realists censor."[6]

As I have argued in this study, sentiments and romantic notions about marriage flourish in the Age of Realism where misgivings about American marriage predominated. Taking into account the similarities and differences between Emma Kelley, Kate Chopin, Frances Harper, William Dean Howells, Pauline Hopkins and Edith Wharton's views on marriage, what I have found is that neither their works nor their outlooks on marriage entirely conform to the prevalent conventions of realism. Many of the representations of marriage presented in these novels are not entirely realist after all. Daniel Borus argues, "The classic texts of American realism boast more than their share of intruding narrators, improbabilities and coincidences, and cataclysmic or heightened moments of life deployed as plot devices."[7] These narrative qualities often associated with romanticism are often employed to some degree in realist novels. When realist texts include romantic conventions, they do not succumb to the old romantic form of writing. Instead, they point ahead to a more modern form. Borus asserts, "In addition to these textual qualities often associated with romanticism, realism also pointed ahead to modernism with the use of subjective narration, a stress on the fragmented self, and forays into symbolism and impressionism, all of which contradicted the realist dictum of an anchored reality."[8] Realism as a genre contradicts itself, but the conscious and subconscious melding of narrative strategies from various forms make realism the genre it is.

Although almost always talked about in conjunction with the romance, one cannot simply define realism and its conventions as the polar opposite of the romantic mode of writing. Realist texts are in reaction to and in dialogue with romantic, sentimental, and other novel genres. There are clear gender dynamics at work with competing genres. Male-authored realism as a reaction to female-authored sentimental romance confirms the conflicted gender politics forming during the Age of Realism. Nancy Glazner defines realism by describing the socio-political conditions that set the stage for a realist movement: "The emergence of the realist literary movement in the U.S. was crucially preceded by the construction of a specifically nationalist, implicitly philanthropic function for fiction, organized initially around a distinction between novel and romance that gradually got rewritten as a distinction between realism and romance."[9] From Glazner's definition we can infer that realism belongs to the genre of the novel, but has adversarial relationships with other popular novel types such as domestic novels and historical romances. Glazner's definition helps us to see that realism and romance as modes of writing in the novel genre. Realism represents the reaction within the novel genre. Given the nature of the propaganda, it was often necessary for realist writers to "cross-fertilize" forms.[10] By cross-fertilizing forms, some realist writers often pollinate or revise old forms to produce something new. Their blended or cross-fertilized forms are not the same as any one single genre employed in the fused novel. The pollination and cross-fertilization of genres suggests that some realist writers are conscious of and openly embrace the politics of fragmented discourse in literature, which had become commodity for consumption.

Common romantic and sentimental themes in these three novels include, but are not limited to, the seduction plot, female virtue under siege, passionate virtue and vice, domestic drama, libertinism, moral questions, masculine notions of honor, and female codes of behavior. Walter Benn Michaels argues, "The true scandal of sentimentality is thus its inversion of the proper relation of life to art, an inversion made possible only by the introduction of a discrepancy between the two terms."[11] Despite the negativity associated with sentimental and romantic writing, Chopin, Howells, and Wharton employ but do away with features of romanticism and sentimentalism to capture depictions of marriage that are faithful to realism's vision of verisimilitude. Kenneth Warren refers to these slippages between romance and realism as "romantic atavisms."[12] These atavisms or subtle appearances followed by resurfacings of romantic convention point toward the inadequacy of one single genre representing marriage. Realism's conventions assist in portraying the tragic flaws of these novels' protagonists, objective narration, verisimilitude, sexist gender roles, and various social prescriptions for marriage that place demands upon women.

Chopin, Harper, Hopkins, Howells, Kelley, and Wharton's novels of wedlock demonstrate the difficulty in defining and categorizing realism from realists in discourses on modern marriage. My study of these six authors reveals similarities among their outlooks on marriage. One sees too, however, significant differences among these six authors' views of matrimony. *The Awakening* and *The House of Mirth* conform to standard notions of realism in the sense that "they portray marriage as an exceedingly bleak relationship characterized by blighted hopes, stunted lives, and a misery that is often unremitting."[13] Yet *Megda*, *An Imperative Duty*, *Iola Leroy*, and *Contending Forces* idealize marriage as an institution that has the power to not only confront but to change issues of moral and social significance. These three novels demonstrate that "marriage was often a communal relationship, joining not just two lovers."[14]

An Imperative Duty, *The Awakening*, and *The House of Mirth*, which are identified as realist novels, employ features that have ties to American romanticism or sentimentalism. Yet realism's conventions are clearly identifiable in these novels, which are overtly suspicious about marriage and its possible outcomes. Skeptical about marriage and aware of its foreseeable consequences, Chopin, Howells, and Wharton are highly critical of the romance for overlooking reality for a more idealized vision of marriage. At distinct moments, these novels also employ conventions of the romance and sentimental novel, but they discard those features to prescribe depictions of marriage as representations of the realist vision of life.

Kate Chopin rejects sentimental and romantic definitions of marriage as happiness and fulfillment for women in *The Awakening*. This notion of the "storybook" marriage, where husband and wife live happily-ever-after, frames the gender inequality implicit in this type of marriage based upon social contract. Marriage, a requirement of consumer culture, is ultimately what causes Edna's suffering. While marriage provides the benefits of wealth and class, the problems that occur in Edna's marriage far outweigh these consumer benefits. Edna struggles to confront issues of autonomy. Though married, Edna is alone. The novel traces Edna's struggles to cope with the demands placed upon her by marriage. Chopin gives a realist depiction of marriage and its functions "as an institution externally beneficial but internally fraught with misery and self-denial for women."[15] Chopin characterizes marriage as a system of domination and subordination. Marriage "harbored inequalities inconsistent with American principles of liberty and equality."[16] Marriage is an unequal relationship where a wife's role is to depend upon her husband. "The story that marriage was invented for the protection of women is still the most widespread myth about the origins of marriage."[17] Marriage becomes a forum for preserving the social order at the expense of patriarchy's influence and power over women's lives. Chopin argues that women's identity as wives and mothers are imposed gender roles placed upon them. Marital entrapment becomes a form of bondage that Edna must free herself from in *The Awakening*.

Despite the realism of Chopin's carefully crafted depiction of the failure of the marriage contract and its consequences, Edna's awakening and death are described in sentimental and romantic terms. The narrator's attitude toward Edna is one of sympathy and criticism, and the novel's theme of self-realization is a powerful romantic trope in the novel. Edna has a romantic vision for her life, but the novel also portrays the realist truth about the limits of both Edna's literal existence and dream of emancipation. Edna possesses admirable romantic values, and we as readers are sympathetic to Edna's need for freedom and self-discovery. For this reason, the description of her suicide evokes our sympathy. Chopin depicts Edna as a helpless victim of society. Like the sentimental heroine, she has been relentlessly pursued by a value system that she does not fit within. As a result, the only way Edna can escape society's prescriptions and expectations for her life is through death. Despite our sympathies for Edna, the reality remains that "marriage has constructed and reinforced hierarchical relations between men and women" in *The Awakening*.[18] The failed Pontellier marriage becomes a larger metaphor for a definition of marriage as human tragedy.

William Dean Howells reduces marriage to the realm of the sentimental in *An Imperative Duty*. The novel clearly begins as an interrogation of the "race problem" with its realistic depictions of the pervading scientific racial thought and categories of difference. The novel's infusion of this racial discourse becomes real through the dialogue of the various characters who speak these racial visions. True to the tenets of realism, Howells maintains an objective narration and enables the character dialogue to present realistic representations of racial and cultural difference. Yet Howells idealizes the manner in which the "race problem" can be solved. From Howells's perspective, racial tensions can be addressed through interracial marriage. His idealized depiction of a marriage between the mixed-race Rhoda and white Dr. Olney is almost too easy of a solution to the "race problem" at the conclusion of the novel. Howells does realistically represent the interracial marriage between these two individuals as one that is unaccepted on American soil. He remains truthful to the fact that marriage laws during this time period prevented interracial marriages.

Yet Howells's depiction of Rhoda and Dr. Olney's marriage as neither flawed nor failed neither resembles nor reflects a realistic prescription for interracial married life. Rhoda and Dr. Olney exist in their own bubble of civility in Italy. It appears that Rhoda and Dr. Olney have a complete disregard for the reality that society's racist values prevent acceptance of their interracial union. Howells idealizes or romanticizes the possibility of interracial union as an appropriate solution to the "race problem." However, there is nothing sentimental or romantic about Rhoda and Dr. Olney's marriage. Their marriage is not a joyous affair. Rhoda, who feels trapped, makes a decision to mask her black heritage and live as a white woman. Rhoda knows that she will regret this decision. Likewise, Dr. Olney is not depicted as the happy husband who has secured his trophy wife. Dr. Olney marries Rhoda out of pity and obligation to an imperative moral duty to save a woman otherwise doomed by her true racial identity. Howells suggests that Dr. Olney is doing the morally right thing by marrying Rhoda. From Howells's perspective, Dr. Olney and Rhoda's marriage sets an example for the manner in which racial inequality within the American nation can be solved. The integration of the black and white races symbolized through the marriage of Rhoda and Olney represents Howells's vision for national unity between the races.

With marriage, there is an "economy of pain" as Sewell describes it in William Dean Howells's *The Rise of Silas Lapham* (241).[19] In her overt rejection of the "storybook" marriage model, Edith Wharton defines marriage as an economy in *The House of Mirth*. Marriage is not about love. Instead, marriage is about money. Securing the most economically advantageous match is most important to Lily as she selects a marriage partner. Yet economic definitions of marriage support the realism of Wharton's view that both the conditions leading up to a marriage and eventual married life itself are characterized by suffering and trauma. Lily's loses reverence for marriage because she is caught up in the consumerism of money, class, and status. The pursuit of these immoral things suppresses Lily's marital eligibility. A marriage would secure Lily's place in society and provide her with the material wealth she desires. Despite this sober and critical realist perspective, Wharton crafts *The House of Mirth* so that we as readers are compelled to sympathize with Lily. If there are any romantic elements at all in the novel, it is the tragic romance ending of Lily's death, and Selden's full realization at Lily's deathbed of his love for her. Selden fails to save Lily from social and literal death because he neither acts upon his love for her nor insists upon their marriage.

Lily fails to see that marriage and not wealth direct her social progress. Edith Wharton's *The House of Mirth* depicts its protagonist Lily as a product and victim of her social environment. In the beginning of the novel, Wharton uses naturalistic language to describe Lily. "She was so evidently the victim of the civilization which had produced her, that the links of her bracelet seemed like manacles chaining her to her fate."[20] Lily has naïve innocence about herself, and she is moral in character. *The House of Mirth* is a realist novel that is invested in the moral decisions and ethical choices that its protagonist Lily makes. The most important moral decision that Lily attempts to make is the choice of a marriage partner. Lily treats the prospect of marriage as if it were an impending contract. In her world, a marriage is characterized by the consumerism of the marketplace. Lily's economic vision of marriage is what influences her to choose a marriage partner suitable enough for her standards of material comfort. Lily understands the provisions of the marriage contract as if it is a rational business transaction. That Lily would consider the intimately private social relationship of marriage as an economic structure suggests her awareness that "intimate personal relationships are determined by or even influenced by laws and legal constraints."[21]

Yet in *The House of Mirth,* one also finds simultaneity of realist and sentimental conventions employed. Lily also functions as a sentimental heroine in the novel. In the opening of the novel, we learn that Lily is orphaned. She is displaced onto family members who really lack sympathy and empathy for her condition. Lily's only clearly identifiable family history exists in her mind's set of memories. Indicative of sentiment, Lily is a virtuous heroine who refuses two honorable men and one dishonorable man's proposition of marriage. She attempts to keep her virtue in tact despite the temptations around her. It is clear that Lily tries to overcome the immoral behaviors associated with the environment of the upper echelons of society. The scandal, romance, and melodrama in the novel are a marker of the novel's elements of sentiment.

Emma Kelley's *Megda* idealizes holy wedlock. Marriage marks the pathway to religious sanctity and culminates into the successful completion of a spiritual journey. Kelley defines marriage as submission to patriarchal and religious authority. The novel's self-titled protagonist must relinquish her autonomous and selfish identity in order to convert to Christianity and receive the reward of marriage. The narrator repeatedly calls upon the reader to pity Meg's depraved condition. This sentimental technique also emphasizes the novel's realist investment in Meg's character interiority. As such, the novel vacillates back and forth with its employment of conventions of sentiment and realism. A clearly realist feature of the novel is the detailed character construction and character development of Meg. Emphasis is largely placed on Meg's character development, and less emphasis is placed upon the actual plot of the novel. The events of the novel are highly predictable. It is clear from the outset of the novel that Meg will marry and live happily-ever-after even though the novel extensively details her struggle to follow that pathway of repentance, conversion, and marriage.

Emma Kelley's *Megda* focuses on the sanctity of marriage where "husband and wife become one flesh."[22] From this viewpoint, women need to be saved by God and by man. Marriage is a God-given right and a sacrament. Marriage preserves both the religious and social order, and Meg makes the right ethical choices in the midst of her journey toward maturation and spiritual fulfillment. The romantic love between Meg and Reverend Stanley is realized through their faith in God. Kelley affirms a romantic view of marriage as a means to secular happiness and spiritual fulfillment for women. Marriage is a necessary step toward a woman's identity formation in the secular and sacred sense. Kelley promotes traditional roles of womanhood and conventional ideals of marriage. Marriage and religion combined ensure the sustenance of social order. By reinforcing traditional gender roles of men and women, Kelley asserts that the social order can be preserved. The happily-ever-after can become a reality if religion maintains its proper place in society. Realistic and romantic ideas of marriage can share an equal existence in a world where morality is at the center of the valuation of marriage.

By incorporating features of the romance and the sentimental with realism, Frances Harper and Pauline Hopkins's works revise or subvert the traditional marriage plot by demonstrating that marriage is not about submission to domesticity but instead, a partnering for "race" work. Even though these novels conclude with happily-ever-after endings, Harper and Hopkins depict marriages that are not representative of the marital love that women consume their identities within. Instead, these novels depict marriage as the pathway to gender equality and racial uplift. "The central plot of marriage in black women's domestic novels of the post-Reconstruction era tended to yield not a story of passionate romance but one of duty, regardless of whether that story relied on liberal or conservative female gender roles."[23] At the center of Harper and Hopkins's utopian marital unions are visions of gender equality, racial partnership, and loyal friendship.

Iola Leroy, often identified by its historical realism, also incorporates elements of sentiment and romance. *Iola Leroy* gives a historical presentation of slavery and Reconstruction as opposed to the plantation tradition that often characterized slavery with nostalgia and sentiment. "In *Iola Leroy*, Harper depicts realistically the difficulties and violence of the Reconstruction period, and finally articulates an inspirational utopian vision of a future South that will be a land of freedom for all."[24] Harper incorporates realism to critique and revise idealized presentations of slavery. She also offers a historical record of instruction for reparation of wrongdoings and motivation for social progress. Iola describes slavery as "a fearful cancer eating into the nation's heart, sapping its vitality, and undermining its life."[25] Frances Harper also uses realism to correct stereotypical depictions of black women and to offer concrete implications of what marriage meant for black women. "According to [Barbara] Welter, marriage was the best but by no means the only entrée into the realm of true womanhood in the nineteenth century."[26] Yet Harper revises traditional cult of true womanhood standards of virtue and marital eligibility. Iola remains virtuous and manages to escape the clutches of sexual degradation and harassment. In fact, Harper depicts an Iola who is free to choose not only whom she will marry.

Like *Iola Leroy*, *Contending Forces* does not place virginity as a signifier of marital eligibility. Sappho, despite her compromised womanhood, manages to restore her virtue and marry. Though the title suggests it is a romance, the central focus of *Contending Forces* is not upon love and marriage. True to the romantic plot, there are two marriages that occur in the novel. However, these marriages between Dora and Dr. Lewis and Sappho and Will come to represent marriage as means of reconciling the conflict of racial oppression. The two simultaneous romantic plots complement the novel's biting realism. Hopkins's idealized marriage plots and sobering depictions of racism are dependent upon one another.

In her preface to *Contending Forces*, Pauline Hopkins attests to her vision of marriage as a promoter of moral growth, source of healing, and state of protection. She writes, "In giving this little romance expression in print, I am not actuated by a desire for notoriety or for profit, but to do all that I can in an humble way to raise the stigma of degradation from my race."[27] Hopkins's attempt to whittle down her narrative as a "little romance" functions as a rhetorically savvy political strategy. What follows after the preface is a considerably "large romance" that presents a harsh indictment of two specific practices of slavery, rape, and lynching. Hopkins's preface refers to the fact that "the atrocity of the acts committed one hundred years ago are duplicated today, when slavery is supposed no longer to exist."[28] *Contending Forces* gives a historical realist narrative of cross-racial blood ties, the raping of black women, and the lynching of black men, which continue even after the abolition of slavery. These depictions of the atrocities of racism and sexism are the backdrop for the romantic fairytale marriages that occur at the end of the novel. Hopkins appears to argue that suffering and trauma must be survived before the romantic ending can occur. The "storybook" marriage is not only possible; it also serves as a reward for surviving the racial and gender obstacles. The marriages of Dora and Sappho are bittersweet, for these two women have endured oppression and maintained their values. They have been rewarded with suitable marriage partners.

Realism is a literature about social change, and marriage is an institution that has the power to change social relations and raise morale. These depictions of marriage not only illustrate the social changes taking place on an American scene, but they also reveal something of vital importance about realist writers and their outlooks on social relations. Some literature of the Age of Realism conceptualizes marriage in a manner that is idealized, sentimental, or romantic. Romantic depictions that focus on sensational aspects of marriage highlight uncommon incidents of marital behavior. This process of converting reality into romance, or the author's partaking in the nature of more than one genre, reveals the dangers of looking at reality through romantic vision and sentimental temperament. Tension between realism and romance in these depictions of marriage is not about genre but instead hinges upon the issue of morality.

By exploring how literature of the Age of Realism conceptualizes marriage, my hope is that *American Realist Fictions of Marriage* suggests how we might approach the task of studying marriage, a worthy topic of attention in American literary realist studies. My approach of looking at varied depictions of marriage as influenced by conventions of the sentimental and romance novels will not neatly resolve all questions in an age where realism and the practitioners of the genre are self-conscious about the relationship between the real and ideal. However, my approach informs our understanding that marriage was both a topic of interest and distinct concern for Kate Chopin, Frances Harper, Pauline Hopkins, William Dean Howells, Emma Kelley, and Edith Wharton. In most cases, marriage literally and metaphorically represented hierarchies between men and women, white and black, lower, middle, and upper class. As I indicated at the outset of *American Realist Fictions of Marriage*, my analysis neither provides a history of marriage nor an analysis of every fictional depiction of marriage during this period. Rather, it represents an attempt to demonstrate that marriage holds a distinct place in the cultural imagination of writers who sought to look closely at the quintessential social relation, marriage, for answers about a world rapidly evolving socially, culturally, and politically.

Notes

1. Frances Smith Foster, *Love and Marriage in Early African America* (Boston: Northeastern University Press, 2008), xxiv.
2. *Ibid.*
3. Frances Smith Foster, *'Til Death or Distance Do Us Part: Love and Marriage in African America* (New York: Oxford University Press, 2010), ix.
4. *Ibid.*
5. Kenneth Warren, *Black and White Strangers* (Chicago: University of Chicago Press, 1993), 2.
6. Hildegard Hoeller, Edith Wharton's Dialogue with Realism and Sentimental Fiction (Gainesville: University Press of Florida, 2000), 203.
7. Daniel Borus, *Writing Realism: Howells, James, and Norris in the Mass Market* (Chapel Hill: University of North Carolina Press, 1989), 17.
8. *Ibid.*
9. Nancy Glazener, *Reading for Realism: The History of a U.S. Literary Institution, 1850–1910* (Durham: Duke University Press, 1997), 38.
10. M. Giulia Fabi, "Reconstructing the Race: The Novel After Slavery," *The Cambridge Companion to the African American Novel*, Ed. Maryemma Graham (Cambridge: Cambridge University Press, 2004), 34–49.
11. Walter Benn Michaels, *The Gold Standard and the Logic of Capitalism: American Literature at the Turn of the Century* (Berkeley: University of California Press, 1987), 36.
12. Warren, 2.
13. Allen F. Stein, *After the Vows Were Spoken: Marriage in American Literary Realism* (Columbus: Ohio State University Press, 1984), 13.
14. Foster, xxv.
15. Ann duCille, *The Coupling Convention: Sex, Text, and Tradition in Black Women's Fiction* (New York: Oxford University Press, 1993), 65.
16. Nancy F. Cott, *Public Vows: A History of Marriage and the Nation* (Cambridge: Harvard University Press, 2000), 63.
17. Stephanie Coontz, *Marriage, a History: How Love Conquered Marriage* (New York: Penguin, 2005), 35.
18. Milton C. Regan, *Alone Together: Law and the Meanings of Marriage* (New York: Oxford University Press, 1999), 7.
19. William Dean Howells, *The Rise of Silas Lapham* (New York: Penguin, 1983), 241.
20. Edith Wharton, *The House of Mirth* (New York: The Modern Library, 1999), 7.
21. Lenore J. Weitzman, *The Marriage Contract: Spouses, Lovers, and the Law* (New York: The Free Press, 1981), xviii.
22. Coontz, 86.
23. Claudia Tate, *Domestic Allegories of Political Desire: The Black Heroine's Text at the Turn of the Century* (New York: Oxford University Press, 1992), 125.

24. Fabi, 42.
25. Frances E. W. Harper, *Iola Leroy; Or, Shadows Uplifted*, Ed. Hazel V. Carby (Boston: Beacon Press, 1987), 216.
26. duCille, 64.
27. Pauline E. Hopkins, *Contending Forces*, Ed. Henry Louis Gates, Jr. (New York: Oxford University Press, 1988), 13.
28. *Ibid.*, 15.

Index

A

B

C

D

E

F

G

H

I

J

K

M

N

P

R

S

T

W

Z

MODERN
AMERICAN
LITERATURE
New Approaches

Yoshinobu Hakutani, *General Editor*

The books in this series deal with many of the major writers known as American realists, modernists, and post-modernists from 1880 to the present. This category of writers will also include less known ethnic and minority writers, a majority of whom are African American, some are Native American, Mexican American, Japanese American, Chinese American, and others. The series might also include studies on well-known contemporary writers, such as James Dickey, Allen Ginsberg, Gary Snyder, John Barth, John Updike, and Joyce Carol Oates. In general, the series will reflect new critical approaches such as deconstructionism, new historicism, psychoanalytical criticism, gender criticism/feminism, and cultural criticism.

For additional information about this series or for the submission of manuscripts, please contact:

Peter Lang Publishing
29 Broadway, 18th floor
New York, NY 10006

To order other books in this series, please contact our Customer Service Department at:

(800) 770-LANG (within the U.S.)
(212) 647-7706 (outside the U.S.)
(212) 647-7707 FAX

Or browse online by series at:

www.peterlang.com